RESTORING BEAUTY

RESTORING BEAUTY:
THE GOOD, THE TRUE, AND THE BEAUTIFUL
IN THE WRITINGS OF C.S. LEWIS

LOUIS MARKOS

Biblica Books
TM from InterVarsity Press

InterVarsity Press
P.O. Box 1400, Downers Grove, IL 60515-1426
World Wide Web: www.ivpress.com
Email: email@ivpress.com

InterVarsity Press® is the book-publishing division of InterVarsity Christian Fellowship/USA®, a
movement of students and faculty active on campus at hundreds of universities, colleges and schools of
nursing in the United States of America, and a member movement of the International Fellowship of
Evangelical Students. For information about local and regional activities, write Public Relations
Dept., InterVarsity Christian Fellowship/USA, 6400 Schroeder Rd., P.O. Box 7895, Madison, WI
53707-7895, or visit the IVCF website at www.intervarsity.org.

Originally published by Biblica.

ISBN 978-0-8308-5745-6

Printed in the United States of America ∞

Library of Congress Cataloging-in-Publication Data is available through
the Library of Congress.

P	16	15	14	13	12	11	10	9	8	7	6	5	4	3	2	1
Y	26	25	24	23	22	21	20	19	18	17	16	15	14	13		

This book is dedicated to

Stan Mattson
and
the C. S. Lewis Foundation

for advancing the renewal
of Christian thought and creative expression
in the spirit of C. S. Lewis

CONTENTS

PART IV: ASLAN IN THE ACADEMY

EPILOGUE: KNOW THY ENEMY

PREFACE

I n the closing lines of his poem "Ode on a Grecian Urn," John Keats makes the memorable, if somewhat enigmatic, claim that "beauty is truth, truth beauty." These five words, when filtered through the life and legacy of C. S. Lewis, provide the impetus and raison d'être for this book. More and more in our modern and postmodern culture these two concepts (beauty and truth) have been separated both from each other and from their individual connection to a divine source of Beauty and Truth: a separation that is perhaps most evident in the twin realms of education and the arts. Even as our public schools move further and further away from their connection to the universal moral code (what Lewis dubbed the Tao), the world of art (whether "high" or "low") embraces an aesthetic that privileges ugliness over beauty, nihilism over form, and radical self-expression over the pursuit of higher truth. As an effective apologist for and a practitioner of truth-based education and as a creator (or, better, a subcreator, to use J. R. R. Tolkien's more accurate term) of his own beauty-enhancing fiction, Lewis is the ideal guide for all those who would seek to restore truth and beauty to their proper place and role in our modern world.

Accordingly, in the four sections that make up this book, I will attempt (with Lewis as my guide) to construct a countervision to the prevailing mood of ugliness and relativism that has so gripped our culture. The first two sections will focus on the arts and will use Lewis's eleven novels as a key to unlock the mysteries of goodness, beauty, and truth that our age has either ignored or deconstructed. I intend the first section to be broader and more theoretical, both in its survey of the problem and in the tentative solutions it offers. The second section is more practical and offers advice to parents on how they might use a family reading of The Chronicles of Narnia to instill in their children a richer, more traditional understanding of good and evil, virtue and vice.

Sections III and IV will shift the focus to the world of education, with the former considering the impact of relativism on children in kindergarten through high school and the latter carrying the critique into the ivied halls of academia. In these sections, I will be guided by Lewis's apologetical and academic works rather than by his fiction. I conclude with an epilogue in which I present my own updating of Lewis's *The Screwtape Letters* and "Screwtape Proposes a Toast." It will come, I hope, as no surprise that Screwtape has devoted his more recent efforts to promoting the Cult of the Ugly and relativism in the schools.

It has been seven hundred years since Dante showed us how easy it is to fall off the straight way. It is my belief that C. S. Lewis (like *both* Virgil and Beatrice) can help us keep to the road.

———

This book has had a rather interesting genesis. It began its life as two separate speeches that I gave for two of the finest C. S. Lewis organizations (the New York C. S. Lewis Society and the C. S. Lewis Foundation): in August 2003 I delivered a plenary address on *The Abolition of Man* for a symposium held at the Immaculate Conception Center in Douglastown, New York; in July 2005 I delivered a plenary address for the Oxbridge Conference in Oxford, England, under the title "Rehabilitating Beauty: The Good, the True, and the Beautiful in the Fiction of C. S. Lewis." I later turned these speeches into essays and then expanded them further into the book you hold in your hand. "Screwtape's Millennial Toast" was written earlier (in 2001), and I have had the opportunity, on many occasions, to dress myself up as Screwtape (in a white tuxedo) and deliver the toast dramatically. In April 2004 I presented the toast as a plenary address for the Seventh Annual C. S. Lewis & the Inklings Conference held at LeTourneau University in Longview, Texas, at which point it was printed, in a very limited edition, in the proceedings of the conference.

Parts of this book have also appeared, in altered form, as freestanding essays in journals: (1) parts of chapters 13–15 have appeared as "The Dangers of a Values-Free Education: C. S. Lewis and the Abolition of Man," *Bulletin of the New York C. S. Lewis Society*, September/October 2003; (2) those same chapters have also appeared, in a very different form, as "Excluded Middle School: Why C. S. Lewis Was Right about Chests," *Touchstone*, July/August 2005; (3) chapters 19–21 form the core of "Aslan in the Public Square," in *Reasons for Faith: Making a Case for the Christian Faith* (edited by Norman L. Geisler and Chad Meister for Crossway Books, 2007); and (4) chapters 22–25 form the core of "Aslan and the Academy," *The City*, Spring 2008.

PART I

RESTORING BEAUTY

CHAPTER 1:

FRACTURED FAIRY TALES AND THE CULT OF THE UGLY

I n a review of the animated film *Shrek*, published in the July/ August 2001 issue of *Books & Culture*, Eric Metaxas offers a brave and insightful critique that is undergirded by an essential element of the Christian worldview that is too often overlooked today: namely, that the good, the true, and the beautiful not only exist, but also are interrelated. The film, which offers a clever deconstructive parody both of fairy tales and of Disney, concerns an antisocial ogre (Shrek) whose swamp is suddenly overrun by fairy-tale characters who have been displaced by a tyrannical king (Farquaad). In return for ridding his swamp of these unwanted guests, Shrek agrees to rescue a princess (Fiona) and hand her over to Farquaad. The audience cheers on Shrek as he frees Fiona from her castle-prison, only to discover that there is a hitch. The beautiful Fiona is further imprisoned by a spell that causes her to transform into an ogre every night. Luckily, as in all fairy tales, there is a way out of her internal prison: when she kisses her true love, the spell will be broken. As one would expect, the film slowly builds up to the climactic moment when Shrek and Fiona (now in the guise of an ogre) kiss. In a parody of Disney's *Beauty and the Beast*, Fiona floats magically upward, beams of light shooting out from her limbs. She then glides gracefully back to earth where we expect her to be transformed, once and for all, into the beautiful princess. No such luck. Instead, she remains an ogre and, we are assured, will *continue* to remain an ogre for the rest of her life. The spell has been broken; she has become what she truly is.

"What is going on?" asks Metaxas.

> Are beauty and nobility and innocence such medieval concepts that fairytales themselves cannot portray them positively? Must not only Shrek remain ugly, but Fiona become forever so? Shall the Ugly Duckling accept himself, and all swans turn into Ugly Ducklings, lest feelings get hurt? . . . Does *Shrek* really mean to say that fairy tale virtues don't exist, or are relative, or meaningless? It reminds me of gray communists screaming that God does not exist and that all human beings need is bread and vodka and cement housing. Did anyone ever believe that?
>
> The old fairy tales aver the opposite; that what everyone knows in his heart to be true is true, that there are such things as goodness and beauty and truth—and even though in this life they are often obscured or hidden altogether, a time will come when the truth will be revealed, when dragons will be slain and bewitched captives will be set free forever.

Amid the great popular and critical praise that *Shrek* received (the sequel to the film proved an even greater success at the box office), Metaxas's voice offers a needed counterpoint. To most modern viewers (whether they be cynical, sensitive, or politically correct), the transformation of Fiona into an ogre is "no big deal." Many would even hail it as teaching children the "valuable" egalitarian lesson that external beauty is unimportant, an elitist, "bourgeois" hang-up that needlessly divides and engenders low self-esteem in girls who can't make the grade. Those who would make such a claim are, of course, well known to us. They are the ones who have systematically eliminated beauty contests from high schools and colleges across the country on the grounds that they discriminate against girls who are less physically attractive (odd that such people rarely, if ever, carry out this reasoning to its logical outcome: the elimination of high school and college football teams on the grounds that they discriminate against boys who are less physically strong). They are the ones who would outlaw black and white in favor of the colorless, lowest-common-denominator world of Metaxas's "gray communists."

Serendipitously, I had the opportunity to test Metaxas's critique in the real world. My two children (Alex and Stacey) saw *Shrek* in the theater when they were seven and six years old. They didn't say much about the film at the time, but when, a year later, one of my students let me borrow his DVD copy of *Shrek*, and I put it in my machine to watch with the kids, they both made it clear that they did not want to see it again. Six months later when *Shrek 2* hit the cineplex and their grandparents offered to take them to see it, they both agreed that they'd rather see something else. This time I asked them why they did not want to see it. Alex and Stacey (who have been raised on equal doses of Bible stories, Greek mythology, and fairy tales) gave me the following reply: "We didn't like the ending of *Shrek*; the princess is supposed to become beautiful at the end, not ugly." I had never discussed Metaxas's critique of the film with my kids. Their response was direct, innocent, and unbiased.

Well, maybe not totally unbiased. As Christian parents, my wife and I have always tried to steer our kids away from movies and cartoons that emphasize ugliness and revel in all the more unseemly aspects of the human body. That is not to say that we have insulated them (they saw all three *Lord of the Rings* films when they came out and all the *Harry Potter* films to date), but we have sought to instill in them the rudiments of aesthetic discernment. Just as there is a distinction between good vs. evil violence (*The Lord of the Rings*) and the senseless, dehumanizing slaughter that runs rampant in slasher and serial killer films (none of which I would let my kids see, even in edited form), so there is a distinction between movies and TV shows that portray ugliness as a thing to be transformed, redeemed, or endured for a higher purpose and those that simply offer us ugliness as an end in itself, that hold it up to our noses that we might inhale deeply and accept its universality and its triumph. Even so, in the heady climes of high culture, there is a world of difference between music that contains dissonant sounds within a greater package of beauty and music that surrenders itself totally to atonal cacophony.

As Dietrich Bonhoeffer has pointed out (*The Cost of Discipleship*, chapter 6), it is not blessed *in and of itself* to mourn or be persecuted; such things are only blessed if they are done for the sake of the Lord and carry with them their own internal promise of that wondrous joy that ever comes in the morning. Yes, we must embrace ugliness, hatred, and lies in the sense that they are part of the fabric of our fallen world and our fallen selves; but when we embrace them, we should do so neither realistically nor pragmatically, but *eschatologically*: with a view to the good end that is to come, with what Tolkien dubbed (in "On Fairy Stories") the "eucatastrophe." In this post-Freudian world in which we live, we have put the phobias and neuroses at the center and pushed "normalcy" out to the margin. More and more, we are doing the same for ugliness: enshrining it at the heart of our culture, while beauty is left to atrophy and decay.

In chapter 7 of *The Sacred Romance*, Brent Curtis and John Eldredge cut to the core of the problem:

> Every woman is in some way searching for or running from her beauty and every man is looking for or avoiding his strength. Why? In some deep place within, we remember what we were made to be, we carry with us the memory of gods, image-bearers walking in the Garden. So why do we flee our essence? As hard as it may be for us to see our sin, it is far harder still for us to remember our glory. The pain of the memory of our former glory is so excruciating, we would rather stay in the pigsty than return to our true home.

As paradoxical as it may seem, we are often more afraid of beauty than of ugliness. The latter hides, conceals, distorts; the former uncovers, reveals, clarifies. Whatever exactly he meant by it, John Keats was right when he wrote that "beauty is truth, truth beauty." He might have added that beauty is goodness, goodness beauty. The truth about us is that we were made both good and beautiful but that we have lost our original beauty and goodness. But the story does not end there. We will be restored someday to our original princess beauty; ugliness was not our ultimate origin, nor will it be our final destination (though it took the redemptive "ugliness" of the cross to bridge the gap between our *arche* and our *eschaton*, our beginning and our end). I believe, along with Curtis and Eldredge, that we all possess within ourselves an antenatal memory of Eden and of our perfection *in* Eden. It is a memory that we cannot wholly shake off, though many try frantically to do so. The fear of success is often a stronger, more intimidating thing than the fear of failure. Better to kill the dream ourselves than risk having it blow up in our faces. Ugliness (like lies and evil) makes no demands on us; rather, it invites us to sink slowly and peacefully into the mire. The good, the true, and the beautiful are all action words that call us to take a quick glance backward and then trudge on with hope toward the distant land that is our true home.

"In speaking of this desire for our own far-off country," writes C. S. Lewis in his finest sermon, "The Weight of Glory," ". . . I feel a certain shyness. I am almost committing an indecency. I am trying to rip open the inconsolable secret in each one of you—the secret which hurts so much that you take your revenge on it by calling it names like Nostalgia and Romanticism and Adolescence." Lewis might have added a fourth name, Fairy Tales, or he might, more simply, have grouped all four names under the single category of Beauty. In saying this, I am not putting words into Lewis's mouth. Of all the writers of the twentieth century (that era when ugliness truly came in to its own), Lewis was perhaps the greatest apologist for beauty. He saw all too well the modern aversion to beauty (though the word has traditionally stood at the center of literary theory, modern and postmodern theorists have all but ignored it), and he understood that the cause of that aversion is finally less aesthetic than it is psychological: a rather desperate defense mechanism to protect our jaded, agnostic age from that terrible Beauty that dwells together with Goodness and Truth in the heart of the Creator and of the creation he made. Understanding further that when beauty is deconstructed, goodness and truth inevitably follow in its wake, Lewis set himself the dual task of restoring (or rehabilitating, to use a favorite word of Lewis's) the reputation of beauty in his nonfiction and embodying (nay, incarnating) its presence in his fiction.

Indeed, the entire impetus for Lewis's fiction may be found in a passage from "The Weight of Glory" in which he discusses the exact nature of that heavenly beauty which we spend all our lives yearning for:

> We want so much more—something the books on aesthetics take little notice of. But the poets and the mythologies know all about it. We do not want merely to *see* beauty, though, God knows, even that is bounty enough. We want something else which can hardly be put into words—to be united with the beauty we see, to pass into it, to receive it into ourselves, to bathe in it, to become part of it. That is why we have peopled air and earth and water with gods and goddesses and nymphs and elves—that, though we cannot, yet these projections can enjoy in themselves that beauty, grace, and power of which Nature is the image. That is why the poets tell such lovely falsehoods.

Among this blessed band of poets and storytellers, Lewis deserves a high place of honor. He may perhaps deserve the highest place of honor, for he spoke up for beauty when it was neither fashionable nor "politically correct" to do so. Throughout history, there have been many cultures that have allowed homosexual behavior; however, until a decade or so ago, no society (Christian, pagan, or otherwise) would have ever dreamed of legitimizing gay marriage. In the same way, though history is rife with eras in which ugliness and brutality came to the fore, only in the latter half of the twentieth century has beauty itself come under attack in the worlds of both high culture and low culture. One hopes that the barbarians who overran Rome could have, with a little aesthetic training, been taught to appreciate the beauty of Roman art and architecture; our modern and postmodern cultural vandals cannot excuse their barbarism on the grounds of ignorance. Their rejection of beauty (and the truth, goodness, harmony, order, and, yes, hierarchy that go with it) is carried out in an educated, self-conscious way.

Even so is it the case for much of what passes for teen culture in the twenty-first century. I came of age in what was surely the most pathetic decade of the twentieth century, the '70s, and we boys back then dressed in a way that today appears ludicrously and laughably ugly. But (and that *but* makes all the difference) we *thought* that we looked good. We *wanted* to look our best, to be Adonises in polyester. Today, more and more young people (and not-so-young people) dress themselves ugly, not out of ignorance (as did we in the '70s), but because they have embraced an entire culture and ethos of ugliness (one that takes in dress, music, art, language, etc.). This Cult of the Ugly (like the sociopolitical movement for gay marriage) is a totally new thing, the perverse fruit of the twisted tree of modernism. And yet, as crazy as it may seem, many today consider these two fruits to be self-evident "givens" that should be accepted as the right and logical upshot of modern progress, the kinds of things that our ancestors would have eagerly embraced if they had only known better.

Against this growing tide of ugliness, we who believe in beauty (and especially we who believe in beauty because we worship a God who is the source and embodiment of Beauty, Truth, and Goodness) can hold up joyously (and defiantly) the fiction of C. S. Lewis. Here we can rest assured that no good and true princess will end up ugly in the end and that order, harmony, and balance will prevail. Here, the swans (to refer back to Metaxas) will not have to become ugly one and all so that the feelings of the Ugly Duckling will not be hurt. Heaven, as Lewis presents it in *The Great Divorce* (that wonderful work which, along with *The Pilgrim's Regress* and *The Screwtape Letters*, dwells in the generic no man's land between fiction and nonfiction), is a place of pure beauty and joy. Nothing may infect or spoil or diminish that joy. The saints who live there in glory unblemished will be finally free from "the demand of the loveless and the self-imprisoned that they should be allowed to blackmail the universe: that till they consent to be happy (on their own terms) no one else shall taste joy." No one there will applaud the ending of *Shrek* as teaching a vital egalitarian lesson, for no one there will be fooled by the lie that the only way to lift up humanity is to drag everyone down to the same level. They will blissfully transcend that manipulation that disguises itself as pity and that makes its appeal in the name of sensitivity and fairness. In short, they "will not call blue yellow to please those who insist on still having jaundice, nor make a midden of the world's garden for the sake of some who cannot abide the smell of roses."

Both passages quoted above are taken from chapter 13 of *The Great Divorce*, and, though they embody Lewis's own beliefs, they are put in the mouth of one of the great fairy-tale writers of the nineteenth century, George MacDonald. Indeed, in between the two quoted passages, Lewis has MacDonald express a truth that not only carries rich theological overtones but also lies at the very heart of all true fairy tales. The truth (all but forgotten in our day and age) is that there can be only two possible eschatons: "Either the day must come when joy prevails and all the makers of misery are no longer able to infect it, or else for ever and ever the makers of misery can destroy in others the happiness they reject for themselves." *Shrek* opts for the latter and allows ugliness to win the day. But the great fiction of C. S. Lewis (The Space Trilogy, The Chronicles of Narnia, *Till We Have Faces*) presents us with a different incantation, one that we ignore at our peril.

CHAPTER 2:

THE SPACE TRILOGY I:

THE BEAUTY OF HIERARCHY

U nlike the seven Chronicles of Narnia, which share a similar tone and structure, the three novels that make up The Space Trilogy (*Out of the Silent Planet, Perelandra, That Hideous Strength*) vary wildly in their generic categories. The first (published in 1938) reads like a fast-paced sci-fi fantasy in the manner of H. G. Wells or Isaac Asimov. The second (1943), much slower and more ponderous than the first, offers a Miltonic theodicy, a reworking of *Paradise Lost* in which Eve does not give in to temptation. The third (1945), which is as long as the first two books combined, invites its readers into a very different world that blends spiritual warfare with the more homely conventions of the realistic, domestic novel. And yet, despite their differences, all three novels center around a struggle between good and evil in which the protagonists grow slowly toward the good, the true, and the beautiful while the antagonists move increasingly away from all goodness, all truth, all beauty.

The fantastical plot of *Out of the Silent Planet* concerns a philologist named Ransom, who is kidnapped and taken by spaceship to Malacandra (Mars). Upon arriving on Mars, he breaks free of his abductors and hides out with one of the three species of rational creatures that dwell on Malacandra: the Hrossa. The Hrossa are an intelligent, beaverlike race of warriors who lack all the trappings of industrialization but who possess the Homeric virtues of honor and courage. At first, Ransom, who is very much a product of the modern world, looks down on the Hrossa for their lack of scientific progress. But as he lives and hunts with the Hrossa and learns their language and their poetry, he comes to see that they possess a deep-seated nobility that surpasses that of his "advanced" European civilization. What Ransom comes to see in the culture of the Hrossa in particular (and Malacandra in general) is precisely a kind of beauty that our modern world has lost: a beauty that rests on virtue, balance, and hierarchy.

In Plato's *Republic*, the ideal society is divided into three classes, each of which possesses a specific virtue: the guardians (who rule by wisdom), the soldiers (who embody fortitude), and the artisans (who practice self-control). When each class performs its proper function, justice is the result. On Malacandra, the courageous Hrossa share their planet with the more prudent, abstract-thinking Sorns and the industrious, temperate blue-collar Pfifltriggi. All three races live together in utopic harmony under a sort-of spiritual philosopher-king known as the Oyarsa (an angelic guardian spirit who also rules the lesser angels, or eldila). Ransom's initial reaction to this social-political-religious system is one of scorn and condescension; he can understand the relationship between the three races only in realpolitik terms and can think of the Oyarsa only as a cold, arbitrary deity. However, these modernist prejudices (and prejudices they turn out to be, though they appear at first to Ransom to be facts) are soon dispelled by Ransom's sabbatical with the Hrossa and his meeting with the Oyarsa. Slowly, Ransom's eyes are opened to the beauty of the Malacandran way of life, and with that perception of beauty comes a realization of the essential truth and goodness of Malacandra.

In *Out of the Silent Planet*, as in all of Lewis's fiction, beauty is rarely something concrete or obvious that can be subjected to analysis and measurement. Beauty is a mystery that must be found, something for which we must foster eyes that see. Again and again in his fiction, the good and evil characters are presented with the same empirical reality, yet see in it vastly different things. Despite the fact that his evil abductors (Weston and Devine) spend more time on Malacandra than Ransom, neither of them is able to view the Malacandrans as anything but ignorant savages. They are as blind to the beauty of the planet as they are to the goodness of its inhabitants or the truth of the Oyarsa. Indeed, Devine and Weston share more in common with the Oyarsa of Earth, who, we learn, rebelled against the Creator (Maleldil). Since the innocent Malacandrans (like the Houyhnhnms of *Gulliver's Travels*) have no words for evil or falsehood, they refer to this fallen Oyarsa as the Bent One.

Of all the memorable phrases and titles that Lewis coins in his fiction, that of the "Bent One" presents Lewis at his most insightful and prophetic. What I termed above the Cult of the Ugly might just as accurately be dubbed the Cult of the Bent. The modern (or, better, postmodern) fascination with and propagation of ugliness marks not some new form of creation, but a twisting and perverting of that true beauty and harmony which God built into our cosmos and into our souls: built so deeply and ineradicably that even the pagan Plato perceived glimpses of it. Yes, it may be argued, ugliness embodies a legitimate form of self-expression, but if it does, then it is a self-expression that rises up out of a rejection of self and the higher purposes for which self was made. In *Contra Julian* (I.9), *Confessions* (VII.15–16), and elsewhere, the great philosopher-theologian Augustine famously argued that evil did not possess its own separate existence and integrity but was a privation, or lack, of good. In the same way, deception and ugliness are best viewed not as positive realities but as perversions of truth and beauty.

Chesterton reminds us in *Orthodoxy* (chapter 6) that "there are an infinity of angles at which one falls, only one at which one stands." While Ransom moves slowly toward achieving that one right angle, Weston (the primary villain of the novel) swerves off in a variety of bent and unstable angles. In addition to his refusal to see the beauty of Malacandra, he perpetrates a specific form of self-deception that lies at the root of the growing tide of ugliness in our day. That deception (which Lewis exposes in many of his works) arises from the bent belief that a single, isolated virtue can be deemed so important that all other virtues can be violated in the pursuit of it. For Weston, that single virtue is the preservation

of the human species, a virtue he considers so vital that he is willing
to reduce Malacandra to an ugly, barren wasteland (to make a desert
and call it peace, we might say) to ensure the survival of the species. In
our own twenty-first-century world, egalitarianism has been hailed as so
grand a virtue that everything (including, and especially, beauty) may be
sacrificed to it. Thus in the name of the egalitarian idol (for that is what
it is), beauty pageants are outlawed, fairy tales are distorted, femininity
and masculinity are either denied or conflated, the canon is purged of
anything that is deemed (by modern standards) to be racist, sexist, or
homophobic, and Christians (who should know better) allow their syntax
and rhetoric—not to mention their hymns and Bible translations—to be
neutered and "uglified" through the use of gender-inclusive language.
And the irony of it all is that we don't even understand the true nature
of that virtue for which we are prepared to sacrifice all. For Weston, human beings are superior to (more civilized than) the rational creatures of
Malacandra, not because of the beauty of our art, the goodness of our
deeds, or the truth of our philosophy, but because we can build taller
buildings, more clever gadgets, and more powerful weapons. For we of
the twenty-first century, equality no longer means what it meant to the
virtuous pagans, to the writers of the Bible, to our own founding fathers
(the intrinsic worth and value of every human being) but a dull and
colorless sameness that, if it ever were achieved, would make the old
Soviet Union look like a fairyland. (Mel Gibson's decision to portray
Satan as an androgynous figure in his film *The Passion of the Christ* was a
stroke of genius worthy of Lewis at his best.)

In the last chapter of the Bible, the angel who speaks to John delivers
this troubling command-warning-prophecy about the times to come:
"He that is unjust, let him be unjust still: and he which is filthy, let him be
filthy still: and he that is righteous, let him be righteous still: and he that
is holy, let him be holy still" (verse 11). As we approach the Apocalypse,
these sobering words suggest that the good will become more good and
the bad more bad. Each of the three novels that make up The Space
Trilogy is, in its own way, apocalyptic, and it is surely no coincidence that
the distinctions between the protagonists and antagonists become more
and more pronounced as the trilogy progresses. Accordingly, the division

between Ransom and Weston (which is grounded firmly in the former's acceptance and the latter's rejection of the good, the true, and the beautiful) grows wider and more unbridgeable in the second novel, *Perelandra*.

This time, Ransom is carried to Perelandra (Venus), not by a spaceship but by the eldila, where he is commissioned by Maleldil to help the newly created Eve of Venus to resist temptation. Once again, his antagonist is Weston, but this time, it is a very different Weston: one who has surrendered nearly all of his humanity and who is possessed (literally) by the bent Oyarsa of Earth. This Weston (whom Lewis calls the Unman) is but a shell of his former self; he has lost even the single virtue of species survival that motivated him in *Out of the Silent Planet*. His only goal now is to pull the Venusian Eve down to his own fallen, depraved level, to rob her of her prelapsarian beauty and grace. He is a loathsome character who, at one point in the novel, systematically rips open the bellies of frogs and leaves their corpses strewn on the ground. He is absolutely dead to the beauty of Perelandra, a beauty that Lewis describes in some of his finest, most haunting prose. Like Satan, who is not only the Father of Lies, but the Lord of Evil and Ugliness (witness the state to which he reduces the demoniac of Mark 5), Lewis's Unman is antijoy, antihope, antilife. He worships a god, but the deity he serves is neither personal nor even a distinct being; Weston's god (like Marx's view of history) is an impersonal, amorphous force that is ever evolving. Such gods (whether they be served by fictional characters or by the makers of our modern and postmodern culture) offer ideal justification for the creation (I had almost said anticreation) of that colorless, sexless world described above.

Luckily for the reader of *Perelandra*, Weston's vision is not the only one offered. While the Unman grows successively less human, Ransom's eyes and ears and heart and soul are opened to ascending levels of greater and greater beauty. All of his senses are stimulated and awakened by the rich fecundity of Perelandra. Much of Venus is covered by ocean and, skimming the surface of those pristine waters are floating islands that move and fluctuate and dance with the waves. Ransom rides and sleeps on the islands, and their gentle undulations fill him with a pleasure he has never known. The "exuberance" and "prodigality" of Venus, writes Lewis in *Perelandra*, overwhelm Ransom's senses with an "excessive pleasure" that is neither sexual nor asexual but trans-sexual: a pleasure our earthly bodies are too weak to enjoy. In a moment of sudden insight, Ransom realizes that whereas the landscapes of Malacandra are essentially masculine, those of Perelandra are quintessentially feminine. Indeed, near the end of the novel, as he gazes on the twin Oyarsa of Mars and Venus, Ransom realizes that masculinity and femininity are not oppressive social constructs that need to be deconstructed in the name of the egalitarian idol but true essences that lie deeper than biological or verbal differences. The former, writes Lewis, was like rhythm, the latter like melody; the one seemed to hold a spear, while the other held its palms open. Between the two there is a complementarity, a balance, a harmony that cannot (and must not) be collapsed into homogeneity. They are the ideals toward which human beings were created to strive: the masculine ideal of courage and strength, the feminine ideal of beauty and grace—both of them equally good and equally true. When we lose sight of that ideal, beauty eventually and inevitably fades or grows bent. The final (eschatological) vision that Ransom receives is that of a cosmic dance in which all is hierarchy and all is equality, in which the center constantly shifts and yet the center is always God. What he sees is more true, more real, more lasting than all the abstract, antihumanistic, "scientific" studies and theories of Weston.

CHAPTER 3:

THE SPACE TRILOGY II:
THE BEAUTY OF THE NORMAL

N ear the end of *Perelandra*, Ransom destroys the Unman, but the conflict between them carries on into the third novel, *That Hideous Strength*. Here, the division between the beauty-affirming and beauty-denying worldviews of Ransom and Weston are ratcheted up once again, not by drawing the conflict even further into celestial regions but by drawing it back to Earth and embodying it in two antagonistic communities. This time, the villain is not a single individual but a secret society known as the N.I.C.E. (the National Institute of Co-ordinated Experiments), which seeks, through tactics that would make the mischievous Machiavelli blush, to establish an efficient, "scientific," omnicompetent state. To say that the N.I.C.E. hates beauty in all its forms would be a gross understatement; at the core of its bent dream of domination lies a disgust for the physical itself (whether natural or human). Indeed, the crowning achievement of its antinatural, antihu-manistic science is the artificial preservation of the bodiless human head of a criminal. Ironically, the Head (a ghastly, perverse symbol of what results when the proper balance between body and soul, physical and spiritual is lost) controls the very scientists who created it; indeed, despite their commitment to atheistic materialism, they pay the Head almost religious worship. But the irony, as it turns out, runs even deeper. In actuality, the Head (and all of the N.I.C.E.) is itself controlled by demons whose hatred of organic life, of individuality, and of human emotion is boundless; their image of a perfect world is the moon: dead, cold, dark, and sterile. The Cult of the Ugly, we might say, with a vengeance.

In contrast and opposition to the N.I.C.E. stands the Society of St. Anne's (alone and seemingly defenseless): a ragtag bunch of quirky, unremarkable believers who live together in fellowship under the patriarchal leadership of Ransom (since returned from Perelandra). They lack completely the ordered efficiency and technological wizardry of Belbury (the headquarters of the N.I.C.E.), but they possess at their core something more vital. For Lewis, St. Anne's represents England as she should be, that marvelous land of poets and dreamers that Lewis, in keeping with his fellow Inkling Charles Williams, liked to call Logres. She is the real, spiritual England that dwells within that unheroic "nation of shopkeepers" that postindustrial England had become. Her virtues are mostly medieval; her love of beauty distinctly nonutilitarian.

Into the dichotomous worlds of Belbury and St. Anne's are ushered our unlikely protagonists: an average, rather unhappy bourgeois couple named Mark and Jane Studdock.

Mark is a sociologist who desperately wants to enter the elite circle of Belbury and who is willing to sacrifice friends and family to do so; Jane is a frustrated, childless protofeminist working on a Ph.D. thesis on Donne who resents her husband's authority and freedom and just wants to be left alone. Through an engrossing mirror-image plot structure, Lewis takes his two protagonists on parallel journeys that draw Jane toward and Mark away from all that is most essentially good, true, and beautiful. Jane, who discovers that she possesses special visionary powers given her by Maleldil to help combat the growing evil, is invited to join St. Anne's. To do so she must learn to give of herself by submitting to the proper authority of God, Ransom, and her husband, and by accepting her role as a creature (that is to say, she must learn to discern and accept the beauty and meaningfulness inherent in hierarchy). In the walled garden of St.

Anne's (in a scene reminiscent both of St. Augustine's conversion and of Lewis's), she finally yields to God the Lover and, by so doing, is enabled to become both a free, unique individual and a full, real person.

Mark's initiation rite at Belbury is quite different. To prepare him to reject Christ and accept the Head, he is thrown into a lopsided room whose function is to disrupt all normal standards and thus pervert Mark's natural human reactions. That is to say, while St. Anne's invites Jane into a world of love, beauty, and purpose, Belbury seduces Mark to embrace a nihilistic, surreal, atonal world free of all absolutes. What Belbury hopes to effect in him, Mark is told, is akin to "killing a nerve. That whole system of instinctive preferences, whatever ethical [the good], aesthetic [the beautiful], or logical [the true] disguise they wear, is to be simply destroyed" (chapter 14). Here, as in all of Lewis's works, the decision whether or not to embrace Christ is not merely a theological one: it is a choice between reality and illusion, between the straight and the crooked, the light and the dark, the beautiful and the ugly.

Indeed, Lewis's description of the lopsided room at Belbury not only offers a critique of the contemporary horrors of fascism and communism (the novel was published during WWII), but also is strongly prophetic of how our own age has slowly but insidiously perverted goodness, twisted truth, and contorted beauty. The description is worth quoting at some length:

> A man of trained sensibility would have seen at once that the room was ill-proportioned, not grotesquely so, but sufficiently to produce dislike. . . . The thing was near enough to the true to deceive you for a moment and to go on teasing the mind even after the deception had been unmasked. . . .
>
> Then he noticed the spots on the ceiling. They were not mere specks of dirt or discolouration. They were deliberately painted on. . . . They suggested some kind of pattern. Their peculiar ugliness consisted in the very fact that they kept on suggesting it and then frustrating the expectation thus aroused. . . .

> There was [in the room] a portrait of a young
> woman who held her mouth wide open to reveal the
> fact that the inside of it was thickly overgrown with
> hair. . . . There was a giant mantis playing a fiddle
> while being eaten by another mantis, and a man with
> corkscrews instead of arms bathing in a flat, sadly co-
> loured sea beneath a summer sunset. But most of the
> pictures were not of this kind. At first, most of them
> seemed rather ordinary, though Mark was a little sur-
> prised at the predominance of scriptural themes. It was
> only at the second or third glance that one discovered
> certain unaccountable details—something odd about
> the positions of the figures' feet or the arrangement of
> their fingers or the grouping. And who was the person
> standing between the Christ and the Lazarus? And
> why were there so many beetles under the table in the
> Last Supper? What was the curious trick of lighting
> that made each picture look like something seen in
> delirium? . . . Every fold of drapery, every piece of
> architecture, had a meaning one could not grasp but
> which withered the mind. (chapter 14)

What Mark is confronted with in the room is an illusion of order
that continually deconstructs itself. Every time Mark tries to rest his eyes
or mind in one corner of the room, his attempts are frustrated. The point
of the exercise (not wholly unlike the point of much modern art, music,
film, etc.) is to get Mark to despair of finding any form or purpose or
higher meaning and to embrace, in its stead, the void.

But Mark is not alone in the room; the Spirit moves even in the
dungeons of Belbury. Rather than producing in Mark the desired nihilism, the lopsided room has exactly the opposite effect:

> The built and painted perversity of this room had the
> effect of making him aware, as he had never been aware
> before, of this room's opposite. As the desert first teaches
> men to love water, or as absence first reveals affection,

there rose up against this background of the sour and the crooked some kind of vision of the sweet and the straight. Something else—something he vaguely called the "Normal"—apparently existed. He had never thought about it before. But there it was—solid, massive, with a shape of its own, almost like something you could touch, or eat, or fall in love with. . . . He was not thinking in moral terms at all; or else (what is much the same thing) he was having his first deeply moral experience. He was choosing a side: the Normal. "All that," as he called it, was what he chose. If the scientific point of view led away from "all that," then be damned to the scientific point of view!

In such a manner have many today been redeemed out of the Cult of the Ugly. The hope is always there that those whose noses and tongues (sometimes pierced) are pressed harder and harder into the dung will rebel against the ugliness of it all and yearn again for that higher beauty on which their souls alone can truly feed. No matter how hard Hollywood, the media, the board of education, the academics, and the lobbyists fight to skew our perspective of that which is universal, transcendent, and eternal, the normal (Mark's "all that") continues to remain.

Let's face it. Most modern/postmodern academics who read this book (or the C. S. Lewis works that have inspired it) would waste no time in accusing me of promoting an ethical, philosophical, and aesthetic colonialism. "What you call the good, the true, and the beautiful," they might say, "does not embody any kind of transcendent standard revealed from on high, but your own prejudices as a white male heterosexual [well, at least I'm not dead!]. There is nothing 'real' or 'absolute' about the disgust you feel at the Cult of the Ugly; that kind of unthinking stock response to ethical or physical 'deformity' is nothing but an outdated leftover idea from Victorian middle-class morality that would best be done away with." To such a charge, C. S. Lewis would both agree and disagree. "Yes," he would admit, "our stock responses *have* been eroding away ever since the Enlightenment entrenched itself in Europe around 1800. But this is neither a good thing nor a 'natural' thing; to the contrary, it is dangerous and self-destructive."

In chapter 8 of his *A Preface to Paradise Lost* (written one year before *Perelandra* and three years before *That Hideous Strength*), Lewis critiques the post-Romantic tendency to hail Satan as the hero of Milton's epic and blames it squarely on our loss of the traditional stock responses to such things as pride, treachery, death, and pain. Lewis attempts to revive such stock responses in his readers not only that they might understand Milton better but that they might understand as well the function of stock responses and what their disruption will mean (and has already meant) to society:

> That elementary rectitude of human response, at which we are so ready to fling the unkind epithets of "stock," "crude," "bourgeois," and "conventional," so far from being "given" is a delicate balance of trained habits, laboriously acquired and easily lost, on the maintenance of which depend both our virtues and our pleasures and even, perhaps, the survival of our species. For though the human heart is not unchanging (nay, changes almost out of recognition in the twinkling of an eye) the laws of causation are. When poisons become fashionable they do not cease to kill.
>
> The examples I have cited warn us that those Stock responses which we need in order to be even human are already in danger. In the light of that alarming discovery there is no need to apologize for Milton or for any other pre-Romantic poet. The older poetry, by continually insisting on certain Stock themes—as that love is sweet, death bitter, virtue lovely, and children or gardens delightful—was performing a service not only of moral and civil, but even of biological, importance. Once again the old critics were quite right when they said that poetry "instructed by delighting," for poetry was formerly one of the chief means whereby each new generation learned, not to copy, but by copying

to make, the good Stock responses. Since poetry [and the other arts, I would add] has abandoned that office the world has not bettered. While the moderns have been pressing forward to conquer new territories of consciousness, the old territory, in which alone man can live, has been left unguarded, and we are in danger of finding the enemy in our rear. We need most urgently to recover the lost poetic art of enriching a response without making it eccentric, and of being normal without being vulgar. Meanwhile—until that recovery is made—such poetry as Milton's is more than ever necessary to us.

Amen, and along with *Paradise Lost*, we need The Space Trilogy, *The Lord of the Rings*, The Chronicles of Narnia, and as many unpolitically correct fairy tales as we can manage to sneak by those most watchful of dragons: the modern censors of "bourgeois" values. If we continue, Lewis warns us, to pervert the traditional Judeo-Christian stock responses by celebrating the twisted, the false, and the ugly and parodying the good, the true, and the beautiful, we will end up producing not only "bent" children and adults, but also an entire bent society. One of the main roles of education and the arts used to be the instilling of stock responses; today, they seem hell-bent on doing the opposite (as Lewis also demonstrates and prophesies in *The Abolition of Man*, written in the two-year span that separates the second and third books of The Space Trilogy).

It is significant that in the final chapter of *That Hideous Strength*, one of the first things that the newly "released" Mark does is to finish reading "a serial children's story which he had begun to read as a child but abandoned because his tenth birthday came when he was half way through it and he was ashamed to read it after that." Christ exhorts us in Matthew 18:3 that if we would inherit the kingdom of heaven, we must become again like children. Could he have been calling us, in part, to return to that simple childlike innocence that takes joy and delight in the wonder and magic of fairy tales—that embraces the happy ending in which inner goodness and truth manifest themselves in external beauty and that therefore rejects as nonsense (as non-sense) the notion that the tale might end with the fair princess being transformed into an ogre?

CHAPTER 4:

NARNIA I:

THE BEAUTY OF COMPLEMENTARITY

A nd so our world is desperately in need of fairy tales that will help revive within us the old stock responses; but where are we to find such tales? Tolkien and Lewis asked themselves such a question and then answered it by resolving that they would have to write the very stories that they wanted to read. Ergo, *The Lord of the Rings* and The Chronicles of Narnia: two works of literature that have perhaps opened the eyes of more children and adults (including and especially those otherwise trapped in the Cult of the Ugly) to the reality and the desirability of the good, the true, and the beautiful.

Aside from the unforgettable names, places, and episodes that fill the Chronicles to brimming, there is another aspect of the novels that remains in the mind long after they are put down: the magic and wonder of Narnia itself. Does not every reader of the Chronicles (young or old) yearn to visit a land like Narnia, a land where animals can speak and stars come down in human form, where fauns and centaurs gambol on the green grass, and where the woods and the rivers are alive? Narnia shimmers with beauty, but it is a beauty that surpasses the pretty line drawings that accompany the text. It is a *felt* beauty, rich and wild and all-pervading. We want more than merely to gaze on it; we want to enter it, embrace it, become one with it. In the concluding chapters of *The Last Battle*, the characters discover that in Aslan's Country (heaven) there is a more perfect version of Narnia of which the earthly Narnia is but a copy. They discover there too the true England (Logres, Lewis might call it), which Professor Kirke instantly recognizes as the Platonic form of the shadowy England below. And yet, despite the glimpse Lewis gives us of the real England, for most readers, Narnia *itself* is the true England (indeed, the true Earth). Narnia is what our world would be if it were truly worthy of itself. *Yes*, we think as we read, *this is how it should be.* Or we might say more simply but meaning the same thing: "How *beautiful*."

Narnia makes us think of our own paradise lost, not just because of its pastoral innocence and fecundity, but because it recalls (perhaps unconsciously) to our mind that part of Eden that made it most lovely. In those blessed days (Genesis 3:8 tells us), the Creator of the garden would actually *visit* his creation. On any given day, Adam and Eve might hear the voice of the Lord God walking beside them in the cool of the day. For the Christian, of course, there was a glorious moment in the history of our fallen world when the Creator came again and dwelt among us, but his stay was a brief one and not to be repeated. Not so in Narnia. There, Aslan, the Great Lion and the son of the Emperor-Beyond-the-Sea, has made many a visit to that beloved land which he sang into being. Turn a corner, open a door, speak a prayer, and he is there, his golden mane billowing in the breeze and his warm tongue on your face. It is his persistent presence, above all things, that makes Narnia beautiful.

When Lucy approaches the end of her third journey to Narnia (in the final chapter of *The Voyage of the Dawn Treader*) and is told that she will not be allowed to return, she begins to weep. Aslan tells her that she is getting older and must turn her eyes to her own world, but this brings her little consolation.

"'It isn't Narnia, you know,' sobbed Lucy. 'It's *you*. We shan't meet *you* there. And how can we live, never meeting you?'"

Our desire for Narnia is inseparable from our desire for Aslan. Narnia lives in and through him; whenever he appears, the winds still and the colors grow more intense. Aslan, Lewis tells us, is not so much an allegory of Christ as he is the Christ *of* Narnia: he is what the second person of the Trinity might have been had he incarnated himself in a world of talking beasts and living trees. The key word here is *incarnation*, a word that unites our dual response to Aslan and Narnia. When all is said and done, the Chronicles move us so profoundly because they incarnate (embody, give form to) all our deepest visions of and secret yearnings for the good, the true, and the beautiful. From the first moment we enter Narnia, we are struck with a feeling of déjà vu, a feeling that grows even stronger when we meet Aslan. We feel surely that we have been here before, that this is the place we were meant for. We feel, that is to say, what Jewel the Unicorn feels when (in chapter 15 of *The Last Battle*) he enters into Aslan's Country:

> I have come home at last! This is my real country! I belong here. This is the land I have been looking for all of my life, though I never knew it till now. The reason why we loved the old Narnia is that it sometimes looked a little like this.

Perhaps the reason we love our own terrestrial home is because it reminds us now and then of the greater beauty we encounter in Narnia (even if we haven't read the Chronicles at all).

Such is the overall vision of beauty that we receive (and absorb) when we read The Chronicles of Narnia. But this vision is not the only thing Lewis has to offer to our modern world of growing ugliness, diluted truth, and tainted goodness. In each of the seven novels (which I will consider in their original order of publication), there are lessons to be learned that can help lift us out of that lowest-common-denominator world that we have built for ourselves in the ruins of Christendom.

I begin with a brief episode from *The Lion, the Witch and the Wardrobe* that makes many modern American readers feel slightly uncomfortable. In chapter 10 of the novel, Peter, Susan, and Lucy (three English children who have stumbled into Narnia through the back of an old wardrobe) meet up with Father Christmas, whose arrival heralds the end of the long winter imposed on Narnia by the White Witch. (Their brother Edmund, at this point in the novel, is not with them, for he has been cut off from the beauty of Narnia by the Witch's dark sorcery and his own ugly spite.) To each of the children, Father Christmas gives a gift to help them in the coming struggle with the Witch. Peter receives a sword and shield with which to do battle; Susan and Lucy also receive weapons (a bow and a dagger, respectively) but are told to use them only in gravest danger. Father Christmas (and, presumably, Aslan) does not intend for either of the girls to fight in the battle. When Lucy is told this, the following dialogue ensues:

> "Why, Sir," said Lucy. "I think—I don't know—but I think that I could be brave enough."
>
> "That is not the point," he said. "But battles are ugly when women fight."

Lewis chooses his words carefully here. The girls are forbidden from fighting, except in extreme danger (Lewis perhaps has in mind the stories of Deborah and Jael in Judges 4–5), not because they lack the physical courage or strength but because their presence on the field will make the battle an ugly one.

A difficult saying, but one that can (and *must*) be understood by comparing it to a similar saying (one sure to make the modern reader even *more* uncomfortable) from part III of G. K. Chesterton's *What's Wrong with the World*. In this provocative section of his book (titled "Feminism, or the Mistake about Woman"), Chesterton argues against female suffrage, not because he thinks women are ill equipped mentally or emotionally to vote, but because society would be made more ugly if women were dragged into the workings of democracy. "If a man is flogged," writes Chesterton in chapter 8,

> we all flogged him; if a man is hanged, we all hanged him. That is the only possible meaning of democracy, which can give any meaning to the first two syllables and also to the last two. In this sense each citizen has the high responsibility of a rioter. Every statute is a declaration of war, to be backed by arms. Every tribunal is a revolutionary tribunal. In a republic all punishment is as sacred and solemn as lynching.

Once this aspect of democracy is understood, Chesterton reasons, we will then see that to give the woman the right to vote (and thus make her a full citizen of the democracy) is to entangle her as well in the dirtiness and ugliness of the lynch mob. Though I would not advocate that the female vote be rescinded, I would agree (sadly) with Chesterton that the twentieth-century impetus to push women out of the sanctity of the private sphere and into the messy, profane world of business and politics has led to an overall coarsening of society. Yes, in some cases, feminism has empowered the female virtues of nurture and cooperation to receive a wider platform, but this (alas) has not been the dominant influence. The feminist of our day (whom Chesterton defines as "one who dislikes the chief feminine characteristics") is more likely to downplay than celebrate traditional female virtues. The upshot is a true Chestertonian paradox: the political movement to give women a direct say in society has helped to stifle the true feminine voice.

Chesterton's warning against the wholesale movement of women into the socio-political sphere is directly parallel (I would argue) to Lewis's caution against what we would call "women in the military." Lewis was no pacifist (see, for example, his essay "Why I Am Not a Pacifist" in *The Weight of Glory and Other Addresses*); indeed, he saw much that was noble and beautiful in the image of the Christian knight. To bring women into this chivalrous male sphere would be to sully, at once, the male joy of battle and pervert the female role as peacemaker. Both virtues are compromised by the experiment; neither is strengthened or purified. All of this may seem to have little bearing on the subject of this section ("restoring beauty"), but it is, in fact, absolutely central. When the masculine and the feminine identities are collapsed into a single genderless gender, the rich complementarity that God intended to exist between the sexes is reduced to a bland egalitarianism: a beauty-killing reduction that has greatly contributed to the growth of the Cult of the Ugly. Whether Paul's prohibition against shorthaired women and longhaired men (1 Corinthians 11:4–15) be considered an eternal edict or a purely contemporary reference, the fact remains that more and more modern women are dressing like men, while more and more men are dressing like their female counterparts. The growth in what we might call "socially acceptable cross-dressing" has further confused and dulled the distinction between masculinity and femininity. And with that dulling there has come as well a loss of both melody and harmony, a loss of that music upon whose precise tuning and balance rests not only much of the beauty in our universe but much that is most true and good as well.

Do you desire to hear again that music that our age has so self-destructively tried to squelch? Then visit a church where the music minister still enjoys instructing the women to sing the second and the men the third verse of a hymn. Listen carefully, not only to the difference in pitch and tone, but also to the difference in soul and spirit as first the feminine and then the masculine voices ascend to the Father. And then marvel, when they join together again in the final, fourth verse, at how well the voices are fitted one to the other and how magically they combine and blend without ever losing their uniqueness and integrity.

Or perhaps move on to the second of the Chronicles (*Prince Caspian*), in which the four children return to Narnia a year later, only to find that a thousand years of Narnian time have passed and that the talking animals and living trees have been driven underground by the usurping, materialist-minded Telmarines. Two of the episodes that are key to the restoration of Old Narnia are Lucy's two attempts to wake the trees and Peter's duel with the evil King Miraz. Switch the genders of Lucy and Peter in these two episodes, and you will find that much of the magic and beauty will disappear. It is Lucy's feminine closeness to nature and Peter's masculine courage that lend the episodes much of their richness and truth. Indeed, it is significant that Aslan chooses the two girls (rather than the two boys) to accompany him as he joins up with Bacchus to reawaken and set free the whole countryside. Their feminine sympathy is as vital, essential, and necessary as the masculine strength of Peter. Unless the two are exercised together, Narnia will remain trapped in the clutches of the Telmarines.

Though Lewis saves his full exposé of the dangers of modernism-postmodernism (with its mania for relativizing truth, "culturizing" goodness, and uglifying beauty) for *The Last Battle*, in his depiction of the Telmarines we catch a brief intimation of the modern hatred for and fear of that numinous, fairy-tale wonder that dwells in close proximity with the good, the true, and the beautiful. When young Prince Caspian (who longs to return to the Old Narnia that his Uncle Miraz has forbidden) discusses his desires with his tutor, the disguised half-dwarf Doctor Cornelius, he reveals that even he has unknowingly absorbed the lies of his uncle. In response to Cornelius's mentioning of the Great River, Prince Caspian, without thinking, exclaims with dread and horror that the Black Woods that lie along the shore are haunted.

> "Your Highness speaks as you have been taught," said the Doctor. "But it is all lies. There are no ghosts there. That is a story invented by the Telmarines. Your Kings are in deadly fear of the sea because they can never quite forget that in all stories Aslan comes from over the sea. They don't want to go near it and they don't want anyone else to go near it. So they have let great woods grow up to cut their people off from the coast. But because they have quarreled with the trees, they are afraid of the woods. And because they are afraid of the woods, they imagine that they are full of ghosts. And the Kings and great men, hating both the sea and the wood, partly believe these stories, and partly encourage them. They feel safer if no one in Narnia dares to go down to the coast and look out to sea—toward Aslan's land and the morning and the eastern end of the world." (chapter 4)

Lewis, the great apologist and fiction writer, was also a great psychologist. He understood, as so few have, that the aversion (in his own day) for fairy tales was as much a defense mechanism as it was an aesthetic preference. The social planners of Lewis's day (like the Telmarines) knew that in seeking to build their secular-materialist-naturalist utopia that they were consciously and willfully excluding the supernaturalism of the ages before them. Thus, if they were to accomplish their goal, they would have to be quite thorough in closing up all the chinks between their own brave new world and that of the past. And the chinks would have to be closed in both the public sphere and the private sphere—both in the realm of politics and in men's dreams. No trespass was to be allowed between the two worlds lest the old genie they had thought they had defeated escape from his bottle and take his (physical, emotional, spiritual) revenge.

In our own postmodern age, we too have had our quarrels—not just with the supernatural but with transcendence, with hierarchy, with distinctions. And since beauty (True Beauty) is inextricably linked to all three, then beauty must be either excluded or (the preferred way) tamed. Great canonical poets like Homer, Virgil, Dante, Shakespeare, and Milton are taught less and less in our schools and universities; and when they are taught, the students who read their timeless works are not encouraged to let the beauty that runs rampant in the works elevate them to a higher plane of significance or link them to some universal, cross-cultural truth. Instead, the students are taught to stand in judgment on the poets and their ages, to feel superior to the "backward" notions of the writers of the past. And as for the Bible, well, just keep qualifying and qualifying, historicizing and historicizing, debunking and debunking until any trace of beauty-laden truth or truth-laden goodness has been strained out. "A young man who wishes to remain a sound Atheist," Lewis warns us in chapter 12 of his spiritual autobiography (*Surprised by Joy*), "cannot be too careful of his reading." The advice has not been lost on our public schools, where educators seem less interested in promoting individual excellence than in forcing all students to fit the same mold—in short, to create a radically egalitarian, lowest-common-denominator world.

Luckily for Narnia, Prince Caspian is able to shake off his "pre-postmodern" education and, with the help of Aslan and the four children, defeat Miraz and his cronies. Over the next three years, he works diligently to put the kingdom back in order. But when his task is completed, he turns his mind to a very different goal: that of fulfilling his vow to sail to the end of the Great Eastern Sea and rescue (if possible) the Seven Lost Lords of Narnia, who had been coaxed into going to sea by Miraz. That, at least, is his primary reason, but I would suggest that there is a part of him that yearns as well to go in search of those very wonders that were denied him by the educational initiatives of his uncle. On his voyage, Caspian is accompanied by Lucy, Edmund, and a new child (Eustace), whose education has been even more starved than Caspian's of magic and beauty. The adventures they encounter on their journey make up the plot of *The Voyage of the Dawn Treader*, a novel reminiscent of the timeless wanderings of Odysseus, Jason, and Sinbad the Sailor. But Lewis, committed as he was to restoring to his age a forgotten sense of the numinous, takes his pilgrims one step further in their wanderings. Lewis does not end his novel until he has carried us to the World's End . . . and beyond.

CHAPTER 5:

NARNIA II:
THE BEAUTY OF CLARITY

I do not exaggerate when I say that there are few works of literature that can conjure the same level of awe and mystery as the
last three chapters of *The Voyage of the Dawn Treader*. As Caspian
and his crew draw nearer and nearer to Aslan's Country, their senses
(like those of Dante on his journey through purgatory and paradise) are
opened to greater and greater degrees of light. They drink from the waters
of the final sea, and it is as if they are drinking liquid light:

> And one by one everybody on board drank. And for a
> long time they were all silent. They felt almost too well
> and strong to bear it; and presently they began to notice
> another result. As I have said before, there had been too
> much light . . . the sun too large (though not too hot),
> the sea too bright, the air too shining. Now, the light
> grew no less—if anything, it increased—but they could
> bear it. They could look straight up at the sun without
> blinking. They could see more light than they had ever
> seen before. (chapter 15)

Like the philosopher who breaks free from Plato's Cave and learns, in time, to gaze on the brilliance of the outside world, the sailors aboard the *Dawn Treader* are being initiated into a richer mode of existence that surpasses anything they have known before, that shatters all the old categories, that makes their former lives seem like lives lived in darkness. Only if such a heightened mode of being really and truly exists can Beauty, Truth, and Goodness have any final or stable meaning. In the concluding chapters of the novel, we are vouchsafed a glimpse of the supranatural touchstone, the standard against which all earthly beauty is to be measured. Lewis the storyteller (even more than Lewis the apologist) takes us to the fairy-tale equivalent (and philosophical meeting) of Plato's World of Being (where dwells the Form of the Good) and Dante's Empyrean (where dwells the triune God). Like an old Victorian explorer seeking the source of the Nile, Lewis seeks out the transcendent fountainhead of that flood of Beauty, Truth, and Goodness that the Creator has poured out liberally on our world (even in its present fallen state).

And if that were not enough, Lewis, after *ending* his third novel in the perpetual spring of Aslan's Country, chooses (most wonderfully) to *begin* his fourth novel (*The Silver Chair*) in the same blessed land. This time it is Eustace, along with a new child, Jill, who is drawn into Narnia for the purpose of rescuing Caspian's son (Prince Rilian), who has been enchanted by the Emerald Witch and imprisoned in her underground kingdom. In a powerful inversion of *The Voyage of the Dawn Treader* (not to mention Plato's Allegory of the Cave and Dante's *Commedia*), the child heroes of the fourth tale move from the perfect clarity and inexpressible sweetness of Aslan's Country into the dull, dark, often deceptive world of Narnia. In order to aid the children in their quest for Rilian, Aslan instructs Jill to carefully memorize four Signs. Once she has done so, Aslan strongly exhorts her to repeat the Signs to herself day and night lest she forget them. Then, as he prepares to blow her from the high mountains of his country into the lowlands of Narnia, he leaves her with a stern warning:

> Here on the mountain I have spoken to you clearly;
> I will not often do so down in Narnia. Here on the
> mountain, the air is clear and your mind is clear; as you

drop down into Narnia, the air will thicken. Take great care that it does not confuse your mind. And the Signs which you have learned here will not look at all as you expect them to look, when you meet them there. That is why it is so important to know them by heart and pay no attention to appearances. Remember the Signs and believe the Signs. Nothing else matters. (chapter 2)

In one sense, the makers of our bland, relativistic world would agree with Aslan: the air of our world is thick and is filled with appearances that can deceive. But there the Great Lion and the postmodern educator part ways. The latter quickly (even gleefully) capitulates to the muddle and instructs his charges to embrace a relativistic world where there are no absolutes, where we are left in the dark, groping for a standard against which we can measure goodness, truth, and beauty; the former turns the eyes of his pupil heavenward in search of a purer light that will order and give shape to the darkness.

In the absence of absolute Truth and divinely revealed standards for Goodness (what Lewis called the Tao), Beauty cannot exist or thrive. Beauty is that which pierces through the darkness and the muddle, that which holds out a countervision to the chaotic swirl of appearances. Yes, stranded as we are now in a world that has been subjected to futility, it is no surprise that we see dimly as through a mirror. But if we see dimly, then we still see. Beauty, Truth, and Goodness, like the four Signs given to Jill, can still be perceived (if dimly) in the thick air of our world. And to the extent that we perceive them, to that extent will we remain on track. They are the touchstones, the counters, the road signs. And they are, finally, more real than the ugliness, the lies, and the depravity. That is not to say that the latter three are unreal or illusory (Lewis is not, nor am I, a gnostic); it is only to say that when they are set over against the original things of which they are a falling away, they will appear as they are: weak, tepid, transitory things.

Near the end of the novel, Eustace and Jill find and free the captive Prince and prepare to return him to the surface. Before they can do so, however, the Witch corners them in her chambers and uses her spells to convince them that Narnia and Aslan and the sun are but childish fantasies and baseless wish fulfillments, while her dark underground lair is the only real world. Weakened by the Witch's spell, the three accept her lies, but their more resilient, commonsensical companion (Puddleglum the Marshwiggle) is not so easily fooled. In order to clear the air of the Witch's foul magic, he stamps his webbed foot into the fire and declares:

> Suppose we *have* only dreamed, or made up, all those things—trees and grass and sun and moon and stars and Aslan himself. Suppose we have. Then all I can say is that, in that case, the made-up things seem a good deal more important than the real ones. Suppose this black pit of a kingdom of yours *is* the only world. Well, it strikes me as a pretty poor one. And that's a funny thing, when you come to think of it. We're just babies making up a game, if you're right. But four babies playing a game can make a play-world which licks your real world hollow. That's why I'm going to stand by the play-world. I'm on Aslan's side even if there isn't any Aslan to lead it. I'm going to live as like a Narnian as I can even if there isn't any Narnia. So, thanking you kindly for our supper, if these two gentlemen and the young lady are ready, we're leaving your court at once and setting out in the dark to spend our lives looking for Overland. Not that our lives will be very long, I should think; but that's small loss if the world's as dull a place as you say. (chapter 12)

Lewis means Puddleglum's challenge to be primarily a restatement of Pascal's Wager, but it also has something vital to say to all those trapped in the Cult of the Ugly. I may have, in the earlier paragraphs of this section, painted the situation blacker than it is. True, the grip of ethical relativism, lawless postmodernism, and insipid egalitarianism is a firm one, but it *can* be thrown off. More than that, it can be thrown off in a matter of days, without a single shot fired or law changed or vote cast. When all those in the grammar schools and the high schools and the colleges and the businesses and, yes, the churches stand up in unison and refuse anymore to embrace the perverse, the ugly, and the simply banal, then it will happen. It will happen when they all cry out together (not as a mass, but as a group of unique but unified individuals): "We have had enough of your attempts to disconnect us from what we know in our souls is real and true; we reject your vision of a colorless, classless, genderless world without distinction or hierarchy or standards; we will no longer adhere to your speech codes or your politically correct jargon or your gender-inclusive language." As John the Baptist in the TV miniseries *Jesus of Nazareth* exclaims, "Before kingdoms change, men must change." And indeed, the change must begin from within, with the rebirth in each individual of an emotion that is two parts defiance, three parts outrage, and five parts longing (*sehnsucht*). And we will be able to recognize those in whom that emotion is stirring, for they (along with Puddleglum) will proclaim to the world: "We will no longer live in Plato's (or the Witch's) Cave, but will set out for that yearned-for upper world where all is illuminated by the sun."

The change will happen when each of us frees himself from what William Blake dubbed "the mind-forg'd manacles," and sets off on a personal pilgrimage for Goodness, Truth, and Beauty. It will happen, that is, when we follow in the footsteps of Shasta and Aravis, the two young heroes of *The Horse and His Boy*. In this, the most *Arabian Nights*–like tale of the Chronicles, Lewis invites us to journey with a boy and girl who are as different in upbringing and demeanor as they are alike in their goal: freedom. The boy (Shasta) is an uneducated orphan separated at birth from his royal father and twin brother and raised by a cruel man in the southern land of Calormen (a harsh place ruled by tyrants who know nothing of Aslan or of freedom). Aravis, on the other hand, is a Princess of Calormen, raised and educated at court to a life of luxury and self-indulgence. When the novel begins, both children learn that they are about to be given over into bondage: Shasta is to be sold by his "father" into slavery; Aravis is to be married off to a rich but hideous man whom she despises. With the help of two talking horses who have been stolen away (like Shasta) from their true Narnian home, Shasta and Aravis decide that they will risk all to escape from the false, constricting world of Calormen and flee north to the promised land of Narnia. They are, in their own way, as fearless and resolute as Puddleglum; no matter the cost, they will place the more real dream of Narnia above the more shadowy reality of Calormen.

Though Lewis clearly patterned Calormen after the Muslim kingdoms of the East (the Baghdad of Harun al-Rashid, the Mogul Empire of India, the Ottoman Empire of Turkey), he certainly also meant his southern kingdom to embody what might be called the anti-Narnian impulse that can infect any state or culture. This impulse manifests itself in a contempt for human freedom and individuality, a prodigal and conspicuous consumption of wealth, and a political structure dominated by deceit and run solely on the laws of expediency and personal aggrandizement. In such a world, power is the only standard, sincerity is replaced by flattery, and friendship is a tool for advancement. This is the reality in which Shasta and Aravis were nurtured and raised; yet, the two are still able to recognize the possibility of a land like Narnia.

Shasta is first able to feel the difference between Calormen and Narnia when he catches sight of a Narnian contingent making its way through the streets of the royal city of Tashbaan:

> There were about half a dozen men, and Shasta had never seen anyone like them before. For one thing, they were all as fair-skinned as himself, and most of them had fair hair. And they were not dressed like men of Calormen. Most of them had legs bare to the knee. Their tunics were of fine, bright, hardy colors: woodland green, or gay yellow, or fresh blue. Instead of turbans they wore steel or silver caps, some of them set with jewels, and one with little wings on each side of it. A few were bareheaded. The swords at their sides were long and straight, not curved like Calormene scimitars. And instead of being grave and mysterious like most Calormenes, they walked with a swing and let their arms and shoulders go free, and chatted and laughed. One was whistling. You could see they were ready to be friends with anyone who was friendly and didn't give a fig for anyone who wasn't.

Shasta thought he had never seen anything so lovely in his life. (chapter 4)

For many today, this passage would be considered as offensive, insensitive, and politically incorrect as the one about wars being ugly when women fight. Surely, the well-trained postmodern will complain that Lewis is here perpetuating racial and cultural stereotypes. Well, yes, he might be, if he were writing a historical treatise or a newspaper article. But of course he is not. He is writing a fairy tale, and anyone who understands the true nature of fairy tales will recognize that Lewis is working within a well-worn archetypal distinction between light and dark, the natural and the artificial, the straight and the crooked. To overlook this is to fall into the same delusion as the producers of *Shrek*, who tragically misunderstand that in the land of faerie, external beauty is a marker for internal goodness. (Actually, it is a bit more subtle than that: the White and Emerald Witches of the Chronicles are physically beautiful, but the obsessive, self-absorbed nature of their beauty betrays their innate vanity and the perverse narcissism of their souls.) Indeed, one of the things that draws children and adults alike to fairy tales is the clarity of their moral vision: the "good guys" and "bad guys" are instantly recognizable by the way they dress or speak or behave. The standards for discernment are included in the "package" and are generally plain for all to see. There is a joy, a vitality, an innate integrity to the Narnians that is wholly lacking in the court of Tashbaan; it pierces through the false solemnity and empty ritual of the Calormenes with the power of a sunrise over a dark landscape. Would that we could restore some of that clarity to our own age: an age in which pluralism and multiculturalism are less affirmations of intrinsic human worth and dignity than they are covers for the relativizing and dumbing down of moral, ethical, and aesthetic standards.

CHAPTER 6:

NARNIA III:
THE BEAUTY OF LIGHT AND TRUTH

I argued above that in The Space Trilogy, the good becomes increasingly good while the evil becomes increasingly evil. A similar movement occurs in the Chronicles, reaching its climax in the final two novels: *The Magician's Nephew* and *The Last Battle*. In these two apocalyptic works that tell of the Creation and Destruction of Narnia, Lewis the thresher continues the process of sifting the wheat from the chaff, the true from the false, the beautiful from the ugly. In the former, Lewis introduces us to two of his most fully developed villains: Queen Jadis, whose all-consuming lust for power has led her to destroy her world of Charn and who would destroy the earth and Narnia as well if given the chance (she will, in time, become the White Witch); and Uncle Andrew, an apprentice magician who would sacrifice the lives of children to further his occult studies. Both villains are as Machiavellian in their willingness to use any means to achieve their ends as they are Nietzschean in their unquenchable will to power and their firm belief that they stand above all bourgeois "notions" of good and evil. For them, Goodness is binding only on the weak (slaves, housewives, schoolboys),

Truth is whatever those in power say it is (might makes right), and Beauty is a dangerous, unpredictable force that must be either avoided or (if possible) crushed.

In chapter 8, they are transported by magic (along with the good characters: two children, Digory and Polly; a cabby named Frank; and his loyal horse, Strawberry) into a world about to be born. That world, of course, is Narnia, and as the six onlookers watch in silent awe, Aslan sings it into being. The beauty of his song is almost beyond description: it surrounds, invites, refreshes. It is, above all, a creative beauty that brings light where there was darkness, order where there was chaos, fullness where there was emptiness. When the cockney cabby hears and absorbs the music, he cries out with joy: "Glory be . . . I'd ha' been a better man all my life if I'd known there were things like this." The children and the horse react in a similar way, "drinking in the sound" with "open mouths and shining eyes." The reaction of Jadis and Andrew to the beauty of Aslan's song is quite different:

> Uncle Andrew's mouth was open too, but not open with joy. He looked more as if his chin had simply dropped away from the rest of his face. His shoulders were stooped and his knees shook. He was not liking the Voice. If he could have got away from it by creeping into a rat's hole, he would have done so. But the Witch looked as if, in a way, she understood the music better than any of them. Her mouth was shut, her lips were pressed together, and her fists were clenched. Ever since the song began she had felt that this whole world was filled with a magic different from hers, and stronger. She hated it. She would have smashed that whole world, or all worlds, to pieces, if it would only stop the singing.

The Word of God, Hebrews 4:12 tells us, is a living thing, "sharper than any two-edged sword, piercing even to the dividing asunder of soul and spirit, and of the joints and marrow, and is a discerner of the thoughts and intents of the heart." Beauty—*true* Beauty—is another such sword; it marks the line between those who would be transformed and ennobled by it and those who would shut it out and destroy it. For beauty (like light, like truth, like goodness, like love) reveals what is hidden; it discerns "the thoughts and intents of the heart" and displays them before our eyes and ears. And when that happens, we have two options: conform ourselves to the beauty or stand in eternal opposition to it.

Beauty is not a thing to be trifled with. The Witch is right to recognize in the beauty of Aslan's song a Magic stronger than her own, a Magic that she must defeat if she is to impose her dark will on this new world. Indeed, when she finally comes face to face with the singer of the song, her first impulse is to cast the piece of a lamppost she holds in her hand at the head of the noble Lion. What she cannot enjoy, what she cannot overcome, what she cannot understand, she attempts to destroy. But she cannot; her weapon bounces off Aslan's head without doing any damage or even impeding the Lion's motion: "And the light shineth in darkness; and the darkness comprehended it not" (John 1:5).

The evil characters in *The Last Battle* (made up equally of treacherous Calormenes and corrupted Narnians) share Jadis and Andrew's fear and hatred of beauty, though they manifest it less in blocking their ears from the creative music than in actively destroying the beauty of Narnia. The first clear manifestation of their evil scourge reaches the ears of the last King of Narnia (Tirian) through the hapless cries of a tree spirit. Tirian sets out at once to investigate, only to discover to his horror what has been happening to the great forest of Narnia:

> Right through the middle of that ancient forest—that forest where the trees of gold and of silver had once grown and where a child from our world [Digory near the close of *The Magician's Nephew*] had once planted the Tree of Protection—a broad lane had already been opened. It was a hideous lane like a raw gash in the land, full of muddy ruts where felled trees had been dragged down to the river. (chapter 2)

To paraphrase an old song, the conquering Calormenes, along with their Narnian collaborators, have paved paradise and made it a parking lot. They feel neither sensitivity for the natural beauty of the trees nor a sense of numinous awe in the presence of the spirits that indwell them. To them, the trees (like the talking animals they have enlisted to tear them down) are nothing but commodities.

But their destruction alone does not signal the end of Narnia. Their assault on beauty is paralleled and bolstered by an assault on goodness and truth initiated by a Narnian ape who knows his Machiavelli as well as Jadis or Andrew. Happening upon the skin of a lion, the ape (Shift) convinces a gullible donkey (appropriately named Puzzle) to wear the skin on his back and pretend to be Aslan. Their fellow Narnians, whose sense of discernment has grown dull over the long years since Aslan's last visit, are easily fooled and begin to follow blindly the orders of Shift, who claims to speak in the name of Aslan. Indeed, so bereft are they of a moral compass, so lacking in spiritual and ethical judgment, that they even follow Shift when he claims that Aslan and the heathen god of the Calormenes (the dreadful, man-eating Tash) are in actuality the same God (later dubbed Tashlan). It is finally their embrace of this theological pluralism and the moral confusion it engenders that leaves the Narnians easy prey to Rishda Tarkaan, a Calormene general who quickly converts Shift into a figurehead and mouthpiece for his own tyrannical plans. Rishda claims to be serving Tashlan, but he—along with his propaganda minister, the Goebbels-like cat Ginger—is in truth an atheist. Lewis's critique here is both incisive and prophetic: modern relativist thought, in striving to make all religions equally true, renders them all equally meaningless. Needless to say, the same principle applies to beauty: if (God forbid) the cultural elites were ever to succeed in their goal of collapsing and reducing all aesthetic works into the same egalitarian, multicultural stew, they would quickly discover that beauty as a standard, as a goal, as a consummation had disappeared.

By the end of the novel, the antagonists of *The Last Battle* have destroyed all that is most good, true, and beautiful in Narnia. Indeed, so thorough are they in their "deconstruction" that they even succeed in fooling many of the loyal Narnians. As part of his propaganda campaign, Rishda calls for a nighttime meeting outside the stable in which, he claims, Tashlan dwells. A battle soon ensues between Rishda's forces and those of Tirian, during which many soldiers on both sides are tossed into the stable. Once on the other side of the door (which passage marks both their symbolic death and their actual death), the loyal Narnians are greeted by Aslan and find themselves, not in a dark, constricted stable but a radiant garden paradise. Such is not the case for the disloyal dwarves, who, though Narnian by birth and "cradle" followers of Aslan, are unable to see either Aslan or the garden. As far as they can tell, they are in a "pitch-black, poky, smelly little hole of a stable" (chapter 13). Even when Aslan mercifully offers them a lavish feast of food and wine, they are unable to see, smell, touch, or taste it: to their warped, twisted senses, it looks and smells and feels and tastes like moldy hay and dirty water. They have chosen the crooked over the straight, the illusion over the reality, and, as a result, they end up trapped in the Narnian equivalent of that ugly, lopsided room into which Mark Studdock is thrown in *That Hideous Strength*. "Their prison," Aslan instructs us, "is only in their own minds, yet they are in that prison; and so afraid of being taken in that they cannot be taken out."

But that, thankfully, is not the last word. Even as there are among the elect those who embrace the darkness and nihilism of their own despair, there is one among the enemy who opens himself to the light of beauty and goodness. His name is Emeth, and he is one of the elite corps of Calormene soldiers who followed Rishda into Narnia. His name (in Hebrew) means truth, and he is supremely a seeker after truth. His great desire to meet Tash impels him to pass voluntarily through the stable door, but when he arrives on the other side, he is met, not by Tash, but by Aslan. Being a true seeker, Emeth quickly recognizes Aslan as the true end of his long search, as the embodiment of that goodness and beauty he has sought for all his life. Still, he fears that Aslan will reject him because he has, out of ignorance, served only Tash his entire life. Aslan's reassuring words to the troubled Emeth are ones that all long to hear who, in the midst of a society hell-bent on perversion, yearn for the good, the true, and the beautiful:

> Beloved . . . unless thy desire had been for me thou wouldst not have sought so long and so truly. For all find what they truly seek.

CHAPTER 7:

TILL WE HAVE FACES:
THE BEAUTY OF BEAUTY

In the same year that he published *The Last Battle* (1956), Lewis published one final novel that offers a powerful and mature meditation on the nature of inner and outer beauty. The novel (*Till We Have Faces*) tells a strange tale that, at first glance, appears disturbingly close to *Shrek*: its central, first-person heroine is an ugly duckling who never becomes a swan.

The name of Lewis's heroine is Orual, and she is the eldest daughter of the King of Glome. She is not his favorite, for, unlike her pretty sister Redival, Orual is ugly. Still, some joy does break through the otherwise unhappy life of Orual through the mediation of two fortuitous events: her father's purchase of a tutor for her (a Greek slave nicknamed the Fox) and the birth of her half sister, Istra (or Psyche in the Greek language the Fox teaches Orual). Psyche's mother dies in childbirth, and Orual becomes her surrogate mother, lavishing on her all her praise, attention, and affection. Psyche is as beautiful as Orual is ugly, and the citizens of Glome, who look to her almost as a goddess, seek her healing touch during a plague. When the plague continues, however, they turn on Psyche and call her the Accursed. In keeping with their pagan rituals (the novel's setting is clearly BC), the priests of Glome tie Psyche to a tree and leave her to be married to/devoured by the divine "Beast." Orual is unable to stop the Great Offering of her beloved "daughter" but vows she will go to the sacred tree and at least give Psyche's remains a proper burial. When she arrives, however, she finds no remains. In grief she wanders to the Grey Mountain, where, on the other side of a river, Psyche appears to her. Though dressed in rags, Psyche is alive and healthy. In a giddy rush of words, she tells Orual that the Beast is actually a gentle god who (though he has forbidden Psyche to see his face) has taken her as his Queen and housed her in a splendid palace of gold. Orual, who cannot see the palace, thinks Psyche is mad and urges her to leave at once, but Psyche replies that she must obey her husband rather than Orual. Offended that Psyche should not heed her first and suspicious of her mysterious "husband," Orual vows that whatever it takes she will "rescue" Psyche.

Up until this point, Lewis's novel mimics closely the plot of his mythic source, the lovely tale of Cupid and Psyche (the subtitle of the novel is *A Myth Retold*), but when Lewis chooses to have Orual not see the palace, he breaks radically from his source. In the oldest surviving version of the myth (that found in *The Golden Ass* of Apuleius), Psyche's sister (actually there are two sisters) *does* see the palace and then sets out to destroy Psyche's newfound happiness out of sheer envy. In Lewis's retelling, Orual's motives are much more subtle and complex. Like Jadis and Andrew in *The Magician's Nephew*, the reason that Orual cannot see the palace is that she lacks eyes to see and ears to hear. Like the dwarves in the stable in *The Last Battle*, she has willfully blinded herself from the presence of deity in her midst and even refuses to accept a glorious gift from that deity when it is offered her. In a pivotal scene just after her interview with Psyche on the Grey Mountain, Orual is actually vouch-safed a vision of the palace itself but then brushes it off as an illusion. Like the Pharaoh of the Exodus who now hardens his heart and now has it hardened, Orual is both unwilling and unable to see. The greater goodness, truth, and beauty into which her sister has been initiated are too much for Orual to bear. Indeed, rather than embrace the vision of

TILL WE HAVE FACES

the palace and participate in the joy of her sister, Orual accuses the gods of stealing from her the affections of Psyche.

The physical ugliness of Orual masks (or, better, reveals) the ugliness of her soul. Though she is, by human standards, a "good" person, and though after her father's death she becomes a fair and capable ruler of Glome, she is, spiritually and emotionally speaking, a devourer. As in the original myth, Orual succeeds in destroying Psyche's marriage by persuading her to break her husband's trust and use a lamp to look on him while he sleeps. When a drop of oil falls on him, he wakes in anger, rebukes Psyche, and casts her out. Though Orual later convinces herself that her motive for separating Psyche from her divine lover was a pure and even selfless one, she is eventually forced by the gods themselves to see through her own self-deception. It was not selfless love (agape, *caritas*) that motivated Orual, but a twisted, idolatrous form of affection that smothers rather than edifies, manipulates rather than gives, binds rather than sets free. (Those familiar with such Lewis works as *The Screwtape Letters*, *The Great Divorce*, and *The Four Loves* will recognize both the distinction itself and the kind of personality type that refuses/is unable to see the distinction.) It is Orual, not Cupid, who is the true Beast, the one whose love is a form of devouring. Motivated by her twisted erotic desire for Bardia (the Chief of the Guards), she works him into an early grave; motivated by her equally twisted friendship for the Fox, she deprives him of the one thing he most desires: his freedom. Near the end of the novel, the widow of Bardia sums it up most succinctly:

> You're full fed. Gorged with other men's lives, women's too: Bardia's, mine, the Fox's, your sister's—both your sisters'. (part II, chapter 1)

Orual, like the Weston of *Out of the Silent Planet*, is a noble leader and visionary—but her soul is bent. She has lost her moral compass, has come to believe the lie, and has dulled her sense of balance and harmony. Rather than attempt to transform her own inner and outer ugliness, she begins to wear a veil that shields her face from view. Shortly after, when she ascends to the throne, she extends that veil to cover her inner face as well. For the next several decades, she tells us, "the Queen of Glome had more and more part in me and Orual had less and less. I locked Orual up or laid her asleep as best I could somewhere deep down inside me; she lay curled there. It was like being with child, but reversed; the thing I carried in me grew slowly smaller and less alive" (chapter 20). She insulates herself from anything that would expose the inner emptiness, blocks out the voice of the divine lover on the Grey Mountain.

I argued earlier that ugliness (like lies and evil) is appealing in part because it makes few demands on us; it leaves us unchallenged: free from all forms of moral, ethical, or even aesthetic conviction, free from the divine command to be perfect even as our heavenly Father is perfect. Orual, like the young, preconversion Lewis of *Surprised by Joy*, demands two mutually exclusive things from the divine: (1) straight answers to her questions/complaints and (2) to be left alone. In this, Orual (and Lewis) is not so different from the citizens of our own modern-postmodern society. We are filled with moral outrage when terrorists attack our country; we demand that the lies of politicians be exposed by the media; we insist that the arts be left totally uncensored that they might better strive for the ideal. But when Goodness, Truth, or Beauty come too close—when they begin to make personal demands, when they threaten to lay bare what we would conceal or prioritize what we would level—then we quickly change our tune and start rehearsing the old litany of all the things we are free *from*. We put God in the dock (the phrase is Lewis's), but we would not ourselves be cross-examined.

In the concluding chapters of the novel, Orual actually gets what so many in our day would like to have: her day in court. She gets to lay her case directly before a divine tribunal. Indeed, *Till We Have Faces* is itself Orual's legal brief, her elaborate justification for why the gods (and not she herself) deserve the blame for Psyche's exile. After all, she reasons, if the gods had only told her plainly that Psyche was happy and safe with the "Beast," she would not have acted as she had, and so she tries to prove it. But as she does, her arguments, her grievances, her long line of fatal choices unravel before her. The truth is Orual *knew* that Psyche was happy; she had even been allowed by the gods to glimpse the palace. It was not her ignorance of the truth but her wounded affection that drove her to sabotage Psyche's happiness. And as for speaking to her plainly, how *could* they? Orual, through years of self-protection and self-deception, has so shriveled her humanity that there is hardly a person there to speak with: "How can [the gods] meet us face to face till we have faces?" (part II, chapter 4). Perhaps the greatest irony of the Cult of the Ugly is that those who join it in hopes of asserting their own unique individuality generally end up empty, lonely, and faceless.

I said above that *Till We Have Faces* is a story about an ugly duckling who never becomes a swan. But that statement is only partly true. Yes, Orual remains ugly to the last (though based on a myth, Lewis's tale takes place far away from the land of faerie), but a change does occur. When Psyche is sent into exile by the incensed Cupid, the god also places a curse upon Orual. She too will be punished; however, unlike Psyche, her punishment will be more spiritual and psychological, the internal exile of an amputated, alienated spirit. But it is a punishment with a purpose. For if she shares in Psyche's pain, so shall she share in her beauty; if she falls with her, then shall she rise with her as well.

In the climax of the novel, Orual stands side by side with Psyche, as the two sisters await the coming of the god: he who has heard Orual's complaint and now comes to judge her:

> If Psyche had not held me by the hand I should have sunk down. She had brought me now to the very edge of the pool. The air was growing brighter and brighter about us; as if something had set it on fire. Each breath I drew let into me new terror, joy, overpowering sweetness. I was pierced through and through with the arrows of it. I was being unmade. I was no one. But that's little to say; rather, Psyche herself was, in a manner, no one. I loved her as I would once have thought it impossible to love, would have died any death for her. And yet, it was not, not now, she that really counted. Or if she counted (and oh, gloriously she did) it was for another's sake. The earth and stars and sun, all that was or will be, existed for his sake. And he was coming. The most dreadful, the most beautiful, the only dread and beauty

there is, was coming. The pillars on the far side of the pool flushed with his approach. I cast down my eyes.

Two figures, reflections, their feet to Psyche's feet and mine, stood head downward in the water. But whose were they? Two Psyches, . . . both beautiful (if that mattered now) beyond all imagining, yet not exactly the same.

"You also are Psyche," came a great voice. (part II, chapter 4)

After hearing the divine voice, Orual wakes to find herself back in her palace in Glome. Her external appearance has not altered, and yet all has changed. She has received a glimpse of the final, eschatological beauty that awaits her. There, in the palace of the god, she shall share in the radiant beauty of Psyche, not so much because she will *be* Psyche, but because both she and Psyche shall reflect (as in a pool or mirror) the greater, dread beauty of the god.

We are all inbuilt (hard-wired, as it were) with a longing for Goodness, Truth, and Beauty, but we must beware lest we seek them as ends in themselves. Cinderella's ugly stepsisters yearn to live in a rich palace; Cinderella too desires this, but only because the palace is the setting for her true desire: to be one with the prince who dwells there. When we reject the good, the true, and the beautiful, we grow bent; when we seek them as ends in themselves, we stagnate.

As long as we remember this, as long as our eyes are drawn heavenward to the One who *is* Goodness, Truth, and Beauty, then shall we all be his bride.

Then shall we all be beautiful.

PART II

THE GOOD GUYS AND
THE BAD GUYS

CHAPTER 8:

THE NATURE OF
GOOD AND EVIL

hough I enjoy, now and then, visiting the local cineplex with
my wife and two children, I really much prefer to watch films
in the privacy of our family room. Released from that terrible
silence imposed on moviegoers, we are left free to discuss the film while
we view it. As the only teacher in the family (and an English one at that!),
I invariably do most of the talking: now guiding the children through the
twists and turns of the plot, now highlighting the strengths and flaws of
the main characters, now elaborating on the theme or moral of the film.
Usually, the kids are eager to join in the dialogue and will often assault
me with a barrage of questions. Their questions range from the simple to
the complex, the sublime to the ridiculous, but no matter the movie and
no matter the mood they are in, there is one question that they always,
always ask: "Who are the good guys, and who are the bad guys?"

Now if I were a good modern relativist, I would tell them that words
like "good" and "bad" are not fixed terms with a universal, timeless
meaning but labels that shift from age to age and culture to culture. If I
were a good postmodern multiculturalist, I might add that these labels

are not "innocent" but are imposed by powerful, dominant races, classes, and genders, on other races, classes, and genders that they perceive as weaker, less rational, or less civilized. But (thankfully for my children) I am neither. Though I am (as a Christian) well aware that there is no one who "liveth and sinneth not" and that all men share a propensity for evil, and though I know too that one man's terrorist is often another man's freedom fighter, I am also (as a Christian) convinced that eternal, cross-cultural standards exist by which we can judge certain groups, actions, and motivations as upholding those standards (good) or violating them (bad). True, as fallen creatures living in a fallen world, we must both accept the existence of ambiguity and refrain from judging the hearts of others, but this does not mean that moral certainty is an absolute impossibility. Indeed, I would argue that we are, by nature, ethical animals, endowed not only with the ability to discern right behavior from wrong, but also with an innate sense that we ought to embrace the former and shun the latter. (The existence of psychopaths and sociopaths no more invalidates this truth than the existence of paralytics invalidates the fact that our legs were made for walking.) Every child who asks his father to identify for him the good guys and the bad guys is participating, in his own small way, in this inbred, hard-wired ethical imperative.

If this be so, and I am convinced that it is, then all of us who spend time with children should so foster and guide them that they will grow to become responsible moral agents: able to distinguish that which is good from that which is evil, that which is virtuous from that which is vicious, that which should (and must) be encouraged if the individual and society are to prosper from that which must be avoided if we and our world are to resist plunging into darkness. If we do not do this (either because we are lazy and apathetic or because we have internalized a modernist/postmodernist agenda), then we abdicate, in part, our roles as parents and educators, as shapers of the hearts, minds, and souls of the young. More than that, we court disaster for ourselves and our nation.

But our task does not end here. It is not enough merely to identify which are the good guys and which the bad. We must teach our children as well *why* the good guys are good and the bad guys are bad. More than that, we must help them understand the true nature of goodness and evil. It's easy enough for English-speaking children to see that the words "good" and "God" and the words "evil" and "Devil" are (accidentally, if serendipitously) closely allied in our language. It is more difficult to define for them either the divine qualities that shine through true goodness and make it live or the satanic nature that empowers evil with its own perverse antilife.

Still, we must try.

———————

Many theories have been put forward to explain the phenomenal success of *The Lord of the Rings* (both Tolkien's three-part novel and the trilogy of films by Peter Jackson). Though no single reason can explain fully this phenomenon, I suggest that a key element in the success of Tolkien's epic fantasy is that, in the face of the apparent triumph of relativism, the novels/films present their readers/viewers with a world in which moral certainty is both philosophically possible and practically necessary. Whether between armies and their leaders or within the tempted and tormented souls of the central characters, the battle between good and evil rages with a fury that is as powerful in its dramatic intensity as it is challenging in its ethical clarity. By the end of the novels/films, we feel that we have not only peered deeply into the nature of pure goodness (Sam) and pure evil (Sauron), but that we understand how and why it is that the characters who are pulled in both directions (Saruman, Aragorn, Frodo, Gollum, etc.) follow the paths they do into the darkness or the light.

Yes, *The Lord of the Rings* has proved a godsend for parents who would open their children's eyes to the precise nature of goodness and evil, virtue and vice. And yet, for all its effectiveness at laying bare the exact qualities that distinguish the good guys from the bad guys, it must (I believe) finally take second place to another series of fantasy novels that explores its moral and ethical terrain with even greater precision and insight. I speak, of course, of the seven novels that make up The Chronicles of Narnia, novels written by a man who not only was a lifelong friend of Tolkien and a fellow Oxford don, but also shared Tolkien's faith in a Christian worldview. Like Tolkien, C. S. Lewis affirmed the real existence of God and his angels, both the good ones who chose to remain in God's presence and the evil ones (or devils) who rebelled against God's authority and thereby fell into a state of corruption. He believed as well that man, though created in the image of God and declared by him to be good, has, like the devils, fallen into a state of sin. However, whereas the devils are eternally and irremediably corrupt, a true and titanic struggle between good and evil, the way of God and the way of Satan, rages in the human breast. Alone we cannot win the battle, but God in Christ has provided for us a way of redemption by which we can be freed from the corruption within and participate in the glorious goodness of God. The struggle defines us, in part, as human beings and is one of the things that distinguishes us from the lower animals. We are the only earthly creatures who possess the knowledge of good and of evil, the only creatures with the capacity both to strive after (and to recognize) goodness and to succumb to the corrupting and finally dehumanizing influence of evil. In the Chronicles, we meet characters who avail themselves of both capacities, who choose paths that draw them either toward that goodness which is most fully embodied in the person of Aslan, the Lion King of Narnia, or toward the evil that dwells in (and possesses) the perverse soul of Jadis, the White Witch.

In *The Lion, the Witch and the Wardrobe*, the first written and first published of the Chronicles, Lewis sets in motion the moral and ethical trajectory along which all the later novels will travel. He also initiates the second, Christian meaning that underlies all of the Chronicles by replaying, on a different world that runs in accordance with a different time scheme, the redemption story of the Bible.

The novel begins when the four Pevensie children (Peter, Susan, Edmund, and Lucy) enter into the magical world of Narnia (a land of talking animals, living trees, and mythic beasts) through the back of an old wardrobe. Once there, they discover that Narnia has been ruled for a hundred years by the usurping White Witch, who has made it "always winter and never Christmas." When they learn that they have, unwittingly, caused the arrest of Mr. Tumnus, a friendly Narnian faun, they set out to find a way to rescue him. They are invited into the home of Mr. and Mrs. Beaver, who inform them that though the Witch's power is too great for them to fight alone, the lion Aslan (son of the Emperor-Beyond-the-Sea) has returned to Narnia and is now "on the move." During dinner with the Beavers, the children learn that their brother Edmund (who, during an earlier visit to Narnia, had been tempted by the Witch's Turkish Delight) has stolen away into the night to betray them to Jadis. Peter, Susan, and Lucy are taken to meet Aslan, who helps them rescue Edmund from the clutches of the Witch and who seems poised to crush her power completely. But there is a complication. According to the Deep Magic of Narnia, the blood of every traitor belongs to the Witch. In order to save Edmund from the Witch, Aslan agrees to offer his own life in the place of the treacherous Edmund. Aslan meekly surrenders himself to the Witch, who shaves, humiliates, and then kills him on the sacrificial Stone Table. The children along with all Narnia now seem doomed, but on the dawn of the next day, the Table cracks and Aslan is restored to life. Susan and Lucy witness both Aslan's death and his resurrection. When they ask him how it is that he is now alive again, he tells them that though the Witch knew the Deep Magic, she did not know the Deeper Magic: that if an innocent victim were to die in the stead of a traitor, the Stone Table would crack, and death would begin to work backward! With Susan and Lucy on his back, Aslan races toward the Witch's castle, where the statues of animals she has turned to stone lie in the courtyard. Aslan breathes on each of the statues, restoring them to life, and then leads his "born-again" army into battle with the Witch. Jadis and her army are defeated, and the children rule Narnia as Kings and Queens for many years, until a White Stag leads them back to the wardrobe, from which they emerge as children again.

Christian parents who read *The Lion, the Witch and the Wardrobe* with their children will no doubt wish to begin their family discussion by explaining how Lewis's novel retells the gospel message. Beware, however, that you do not reduce it to *only* an allegory of the Christian story. Emphasize that the characters who act and interact in the novel are "real" characters whose lives have their own integrity and meaning within the frame of the story. Let the drama of the tale (and the luminous "person" of Aslan) exert its full impact on your children before you begin to "unpack" its underlying Christian message. You might explain to them that (to paraphrase a comment from Lewis himself) Aslan is not simply an allegory (or representation) of Christ, but that Aslan is what the Son of God (the second person of the Trinity) might have been like had he been incarnated on a magical world of talking animals, living trees, and mythic beasts. If you keep this in mind, though, I think it is "safe" to suggest some simple parallels between the novel and the gospel.

Edmund, like Adam, has committed an act of disobedient treachery against those whom he should love. (As traitor, he also resembles Judas, but I think the link to Adam is finally more fruitful.) As a result of his sinful choice, he is cut off from the fellowship of both his family and Aslan and becomes the pawn of the White Witch. Just so, we, like Edmund, are separated from God by sin, and our lives are forfeit to Satan (who, like Jadis, is also the ruler of our fallen world). The situation is one that we (like Edmund) cannot remedy on our own. Our salvation from death (and redemption from the just claim of Satan) can come only by God (the Emperor-Beyond-the-Sea) sending his Son (Aslan) to invade our "enemy-occupied" world (Aslan is "on the move") and to take our punishment upon himself by willingly offering up his life on the cross (the Stone Table). But the story does not end there. Christ (like Aslan) rises again from the dead and thus sets in motion not only our own salvation but also the whole world's salvation.

If the children are still with you, you might try moving on to more sophisticated theological concepts. It is no coincidence that Aslan is killed on a Stone Table that then cracks in two when he rises again. On the simplest level, the cracked Table recalls the stone that rolled away from the tomb at the resurrection of Christ. On a deeper level, it recalls the veil in the temple, which miraculously tore in two from top to bottom when Christ was crucified. Historically, the veil separated the people from the Holy of Holies, that most sacred of places which once had held the ark of the covenant and into which the high priest alone could enter, and even then on only one day of the year (the Day of Atonement). Since the death of Christ, we no longer need the veil or the temple or the high priest; through the blood of Christ shed on the cross, we are all granted direct access to the Holy God. On a yet deeper level, the Stone Table recalls the tablets of the law on which God wrote the Ten Commandments. In the Old Testament (before the coming of Christ), the covenant between God and his people (the Jews) was mediated by the law of Moses, a law that included the intractable rule that the punishment for sin is death (the Deep Magic). But when Christ died and rose again (the Deeper Magic), the legalistic and condemnatory force of the old law/covenant was broken, and grace took its place: a grace that cements the new covenant (or testament) between God and the church.

Finally, if you wish to ratchet it up one more notch, you might discuss how the scene in which Aslan breathes on the statues and restores them to life offers a powerful picture of what it means to have new life in Christ. Christ (like Aslan) did not simply come back from the dead in the sense of being resuscitated (as Lazarus was); he went *through* death and came out on the other side. In the New Testament, this is made clear by the fact that Christ now wears a resurrection body that can "walk through walls" and appear and disappear at will. In Lewis's novel, this is captured in a single powerful detail. Before Aslan is killed, his hair and mane are shaved off. When he resurrects and appears to Susan and Lucy (as Jesus did to the Marys), not only is his mane restored; it is richer and more golden than before. It is suggested (though not clearly stated) in the novel that before his death/resurrection, Aslan did not have the power to breathe on statues and restore them to life. But now that he has himself conquered death and risen anew, he has the power to share that life with anyone he wishes. Just so, the risen Christ has the power to grant us, here and now, a new and more vital life and, in the age to come, a resurrection body like unto his own.

CHAPTER 9:

FURTHER UP
AND FURTHER DOWN

S o far so good. If your children get this much out of the novel, they are doing quite well. But I would strongly urge you not to end your discussion here. *The Lion, the Witch and the Wardrobe* offers the opportunity not only to identify for your children the ultimate good guy (Aslan, Christ) and bad guy (the White Witch, Satan), but also, as I suggested earlier, to delve more deeply into the full and true nature of good and evil. Though one can start such a discussion by focusing first on evil and then moving on to good, I would suggest starting with goodness instead. In our culture (and, alas, in our churches), we too often promote a negative view of goodness; we think of it merely as the absence of evil, of a simple restraint from the temptations of the flesh. The truth, of course, is completely the opposite. It is evil that is the negative thing, the falling away, the perversion of a primal and positive goodness. As Lewis teaches us in his nonfiction, there is no such thing as perfect evil: if evil *were* ever to succeed in becoming only evil, it would cease to exist. The hole in a shirt is nothing without the shirt; just so, evil (which Augustine defines as the privation of good) can exist only inasmuch as it preys on and defiles and corrupts something good that God made. (If your children are old enough, here is the time to explain to them that sex is not a bad thing that we must utterly resist in the name of a negative purity, but that sexuality/intimacy is a gift of God that we must be careful not to misuse or defile.)

There are few characters in literature who embody positive goodness more powerfully than Aslan. In his presence, the children feel at once a sense of joy and fear, an ecstasy mingled with terror, an intimation of both the actively sublime and the passively beautiful. Aslan is neither a pretty object to be placed on a shelf, nor a tame pet to be domesticated. He is fierce, wild, and unpredictable. The first time the children hear his name, they are taken out of themselves (the literal meaning of the word *ecstasy*); when they meet him in person, their legs tremble beneath them. Yes, they are told by the Beavers, he is good and just and loving, but he is by no means safe. He is to be trusted and loved, but not to be trifled with. One might as well try to pet a lion or dance with a tornado. After Aslan rises from the dead and shows himself to the girls, he warns them that they must put their fingers in their ears, for he feels a roar welling up inside of him. Susan and Lucy do as they are told; then, Lewis describes, "Aslan stood up, and when he opened his mouth to roar, his face became so terrible that [the girls] did not dare to look at it. And they saw all the trees in front of him bend before the blast of his roaring as grass bends in a meadow before the wind" (chapter 15). The newly risen Aslan is like a hurricane unleashed, a force that both tears away the death imposed on Narnia by the White Witch and ushers in renewal and redemption. In its wake, spring returns to Narnia.

But Aslan's power does not manifest itself only in his triumph over death, winter, and the Witch. When Aslan surrenders himself to Jadis at the Stone Table, he does so not out of weakness (he is no guilt-ridden doormat) but out of a position of compassionate strength. The kinetic energy released at his resurrection is there throughout the novel in potential form, like a coiled spring ever ready to snap. From the very moment that Aslan learns of the treachery of Edmund, he knows what he must do. The tragic knowledge of his own coming sacrifice weighs heavily on Aslan, but he carries it through to the end, as only one who knows his purpose and embraces it can do. When, after the first shock of Aslan's humiliation passes, and Lucy can bear to look up at him again, she realizes, to her surprise, that "the shorn face of Aslan [now looks] to her braver, and more beautiful, and more patient than ever" (chapter 14).

Lewis felt that the children and adults of his day had lost what he liked to call (after Rudolph Otto) a sense of the numinous: a sense of awe or dread that mingles terror with beauty and that makes one feel small and insignificant, but not repulsive or suicidal, in the face of a transcendent force. It is the dulling of this sense in Lewis's day—and our own—that accounts for what many modern writers have called the loss of the sacred. Lewis was truly concerned (as we should all be) that modern children could no longer conceive of something being both wonderful and terrible, fun and serious at the same time. Aslan *is* that very something, and it was Lewis's hope that if children learned to feel a sense of the numinous in the presence of Aslan, they could later transfer that feeling to its proper object: the triune God of the Bible. I can attest to the power of the Chronicles to do just that every time my family takes a long driving trip and listens to the excellent radio play versions of the Chronicles produced by Focus on the Family. As we listen, the children (or my wife and I) might start talking or drifting into other thoughts, but when Aslan bounds on to the scene, the interior of the car grows still, and a strange awe resonates in the air. A faint but real echo of that ecstatic dread that Isaiah and John felt when they stood before the throne room of God falls upon us and draws us out of our mundane concerns.

Those characters in the novel who hearken to the numinous presence of Aslan and allow it to transform them find that they are capable of acts of great courage and mercy. Even the treacherous Edmund, changed from within by the awesome love of Aslan, shows himself willing to sacrifice his own life for his friends and for Narnia in the final battle with the Witch. Too often our modern icons of goodness are too weak, passive, and restrained to appeal to the young. Through Aslan, they can learn (and *experience*) a richer, divine goodness that shatters all boundaries and that has the power to restore, renew, and revive.

When set over against the pulsating goodness of Aslan, the evil of the White Witch and her minions seems, finally, a paltry, petty, lifeless thing. In *The Screwtape Letters*, the senior devil, Screwtape, explains to his nephew, Wormwood (a young, naive tempter), that the ultimate difference between God and Satan is that the latter wants cattle that he can use for food, while the former wants servants whom he can turn into sons. In the triangle that forms between Aslan, Edmund, and the White Witch, we see this truth played out. Jadis tempts Edmund to betray his siblings by promising him that he will reign with her as a Prince and that he will eat all the Turkish Delight that he wants. In reality, the Witch transforms Edmund into a slave whom she insults, abuses, and feeds on stale bread and water. Edmund thinks that the Witch will make him wiser, stronger, and better than his siblings; instead, she reduces him to a thing of little value and no purpose. Under her evil influence, he comes to hate not only his siblings and Aslan but also himself. Worse yet, his gluttonous desire for the Witch's Turkish Delight has the effect of ruining for him all other types of joy. As Lewis so simply but profoundly puts it: "There's nothing that spoils the taste of good ordinary food half so much as the memory of bad magic food" (chapter 9).

It is a sad fact of humanity that most of us (whatever the age or culture in which we were raised) grow up believing a terrible lie: namely, whereas Satan wants to set us free to be truly ourselves, Christ wants to crush our personality and make us all the same. Allied to this is an equally false belief that Christ is a cosmic killjoy, a joyless Puritan who hates all forms of merriment, revelry, and indulgence. In a memorable yet easily overlooked scene in *The Lion, the Witch and the Wardrobe*, Lewis gives the lie to this satanic propaganda, showing that it is, in fact, the Devil (and not Christ) who is the real killjoy.

Even before his resurrection, Aslan, simply by his presence in Narnia, causes the long winter of the Witch to begin to thaw. In tandem with this breaking of the Witch's icy grip, Aslan's appearance also brings into Narnia the jolly figure of Father Christmas. While on her way to overtake Peter, Susan, and Lucy before they can reach Aslan, the Witch comes upon a party of talking animals who are partaking of a feast provided for them by Father Christmas. When she spies them, the Witch is *not* pleased that they are drinking wine and stuffing themselves with food. Indeed, her response to them is identical to what most Christians *think* (wrongly) is God's default reaction to our earthly pleasures: "What is the meaning of all this gluttony, this waste, this self-indulgence? Where did you get all these things?" (chapter 11). If the Witch had her way, Narnia would not be a land of gluttony and dipsomania, but a cold, dead world inhabited by automatons whose joy and life and potential for growth have been swallowed up by her devouring envy and pride. And for those who refuse to be so emptied of their vitality, the Witch simply turns them into stone statues, which is exactly what she does to the "party animals" she meets on the road.

Though most evangelical Christians point to John 3:16 as their favorite verse, mine has always come from a later chapter in John: from his beautiful discourse of the Good Shepherd (10:1–18). In verse 10 of this passage, Christ describes, in the most precise way, what the difference is between his own goodness and the evil of Satan (the thief): "The thief cometh not, but for to steal, and to kill, and to destroy: I am come that they might have life, and that they might have it more abundantly." In its depiction not only of Aslan and the White Witch but also of those characters who fall under their sway, *The Lion, the Witch and the Wardrobe* offers a veritable dramatization of this key verse. And, by so doing, it offers as well one of the classic responses to that perennial question: "Who are the good guys, and who are the bad guys?"

―――――――

Those who have read only *The Lion, the Witch and the Wardrobe* and who have recognized its allegorical link to the gospel story often wonder how (and perhaps why) Lewis managed to retell that story six more times in the remaining Chronicles. The answer, of course, is that he did not. Rather than revisit the Easter accounts of the four gospels, Lewis follows the cue of the other books of the Bible and of the weighty tradition of Christian (and pre-Christian) literature. That is to say, he explores in the other chronicles the choices that lie before those who live in a moral universe in which good has triumphed but in which evil still remains.

As most (though, alas, not all) lovers of The Chronicles of Narnia are

well aware, the seven novels are unfortunately published today in an order that differs from their original order of publication: an ordering that
follows the internal chronology of Narnian history. Thus, *The Magician's
Nephew* (originally published sixth), because it deals with the creation of
Narnia, is placed first in the new ordering. Likewise, *The Horse and His
Boy* (originally published fifth) is placed between *The Lion, the Witch and
the Wardrobe* and *Prince Caspian* because it takes place during the reign
of High King Peter, thus overlapping with the last chapter of *The Lion,
the Witch and the Wardrobe*. There are many reasons to prefer the original
ordering, but the one that concerns us here was first noted, I believe, by
Paul Ford in the introduction to his *Companion to Narnia*. Ford reasons
(rightly, I think) that if the Chronicles are to be seen as reworking in the
genre of fantasy the sacred history of the Bible, then it makes the most
sense to begin with the salvation story that lies at the crux of that history.
Just so did the church fathers who decided on the arrangement of the
New Testament choose rightly when they placed the gospel narratives
first in order, even though they knew that the Epistles of Paul had been
written earlier. As Christians we read the Bible—both the Old Testament
and the New Testament—in the light of the death and resurrection of
Christ; in the same way, it is best to read the seven chronicles (including *The Magician's Nephew*) with an eye to Aslan's victory over death,
treachery, and the White Witch.

It is against this backdrop that we shall now explore, chronicle by
chronicle, the choices made by those characters who act out their parts
for good or for ill in the shadow of the risen lion. Indeed, as my focus will
be *on* those choices, I shall say relatively little about Aslan in the chapters
that follow. Though Aslan stands at the moral center of all the tales, to
ask a child (or adult) to live up to his Pure Goodness would be far too
daunting. For that reason, I shall concern myself with the more "human"
examples of good and evil that provide the Chronicles with much of their
interest, conflict, and moral power.

CHAPTER 10:

HEROES AND VILLAINS

C ompared to the White Witch, the bad guy of *Prince Caspian*, Uncle Miraz, is a more standard villain, recognizable from both fiction and history. He is the power-hungry usurper who, like Claudius in *Hamlet*, kills his own brother in order to steal his throne. He even proves willing, as have many tyrants throughout history, to kill his young, innocent nephew Caspian as a way of securing his own dynastic line. Miraz is one in a long line of Telmarine Kings (some, like Caspian's father, good, but most of them bad) who have seized control of Narnia and driven the talking beasts underground. In many ways, they have transformed the once innocent and carefree Narnia into a police state ruled by fear and suspicion. Again, the situation is a familiar one, but Lewis adds to it a subtle twist that brings out more fully the precise *nature* of Miraz's evil. You see, it is not enough for Miraz that he and his heirs have expelled the talking beasts (and with them, their messianic hope in Aslan). Miraz's true goal is to obliterate even the memory of Aslan and the talking beasts by converting those sacred memories into lies and superstitions. If he has his way, the history of Narnia will be so rewritten as to leave out both the sacrifice and resurrection of Aslan and the ancient faith and deeds of his followers. He is, to use the language of our own world, a secular humanist with a vengeance! When the young Caspian asks him about the "old stories" of Aslan and the four Kings and Queens, Miraz ridicules the boy and attempts to strangle his yearning for the old days.

Despite, however, the concerted attempts of the evil Miraz to "demythologize" his nephew's beliefs, the good Caspian keeps alive his yearnings for the real Narnia of old and risks everything to bring it back. Caspian is innocent without being naive, idealistic without being impotent; he does not seek after some utopian pie in the sky, but a revival of the true spirit of Narnia. He is an excellent role model for children who must face a modern world rife with cynicism and nay-saying, and his struggle with Miraz offers an ideal opportunity for the discerning parent to expose for his child one of the key attributes of evil in our world. Miraz is a villain, the parent must teach his child, not because his beliefs differ from those of Caspian, but because he desires to crush all belief to achieve his ends. He is like the thief in John 10 (see chapter 9) who comes only to steal, kill, and destroy. His revisionist campaign seeks not to bring the light of knowledge but to snuff it out.

The Miraz-Caspian conflict offers the perfect teachable moment for instruction in the nature of good and evil, but it is not the only conflict that offers itself for such a purpose. There is a second, less obvious conflict that also has much to say about good and evil and how those opposing states are related to the central issue of belief. While fleeing from Miraz, Caspian falls into the company of a talking badger named Trufflehunter, a red dwarf named Trumpkin, and a black dwarf named Nikabrik. At first, Trumpkin and Nikabrik seem to be very similar types; neither of them believes (in contrast to the pious Trufflehunter) in Aslan or the ancient tales of the four Kings and Queens, and neither of them is much disposed to trust the Telmarine Caspian. As the story progresses, however, we learn that the unbelief of Trumpkin and Nikabrik is qualitatively different. Nikabrik's unbelief is based on pride, despair, and a refusal to embrace joy; Trumpkin's, on the other hand, is based more on caution, ignorance, and a generous dose of stubbornness. Trumpkin *can't* believe because he has never encountered the presence of Aslan and because he fears that if Caspian and his army place all their faith in old stories, they will be destroyed by the forces of Miraz. Nikabrik *won't* believe because he has grown cold and dead on the inside and because he is motivated by revenge and hatred rather than by a love for Narnia and her talking beasts.

The true distinction between their characters becomes evident after Caspian blows a magic horn that promises to bring help (by, as it turns out, drawing Peter, Susan, Edmund, and Lucy back into Narnia) and asks for a volunteer to travel quickly to Cair Paravel to see if the help has arrived. Nikabrik categorically refuses the task because he feels he must remain behind to watch out for the partisan interests of himself and his fellow black dwarfs. Trumpkin, on the other hand, immediately accepts Caspian's commission, not because he believes in the magic of the horn (in matter of fact, he does not) but because he knows his duty to his King. Trumpkin's heart is both open and noble, and when, eventually, he comes face to face with Aslan, he believes and proves faithful. Nikabrik's heart is closed and defensive, and he is eventually destroyed in the midst of an evil attempt to bring back the White Witch by black magic to help him fight Miraz. It is as wonderful to watch Trumpkin slowly emerge into the light, as it is frightening to watch Nikabrik slowly fall into darkness. Children (and their parents) need to understand the vital lesson that it is not where we begin but where we end that counts. There are some (to paraphrase the moral of one of Jesus' parables) who initially say yes to God but then do not do what he says when the time of decision comes; there are others who run from God and refuse his call but who turn and do his will in the end. Trumpkin (like the jaded prostitutes and worldly-wise tax collectors who accepted Jesus) is a member of the second group; Nikabrik (like the self-righteous Pharisees who rejected him) is a member of the first. Belief is not just a matter of the head, but of the heart and the hand. There are only two kinds of people in the world . . .

———

Both Caspian and Trumpkin are memorable characters on account of the courage and nobility of their hearts. But both are eclipsed by another Narnian whose chivalric goodness and valor are equal to that of good King Arthur himself. I speak, of course, of Reepicheep the mouse, who first appears in *Prince Caspian* as one of the soldiers in Caspian's army, but who takes on an even more central role in *The Voyage of the Dawn Treader*. The setting is three years after Caspian's defeat of Miraz and his ascent to the throne of Narnia. With the help of Trumpkin, Caspian has set all to rights in his kingdom and now sails to the far Eastern Sea in search of seven lost Narnian lords who had been sent on wild-goose chases by Miraz in hopes that they would never return. Though he and his crew have undertaken the journey to carry out this royal mission (and perhaps have a little adventure along the way!), Reepicheep sails for a very different reason. He hopes that by sailing east to the end of the world, he will arrive at Aslan's Country and thus achieve his heart's desire. That is to say, Lewis's great warrior mouse is also a great mystic; like Sir Galahad (or Lancelot before his fall), Reepicheep possesses in full the two chivalric virtues of courage and purity.

Needless to say, such characters are few and far between in our modern world. Children in our day are too often presented with heroes who are *either* brave and strong *or* meek and humble. We have lost the old Christian sense that a hero can be *both* manly and religious, vigorous and virtuous, pugnacious and pious. How many young boys today have a father they can imagine standing up undaunted before an oppressor in one moment and kneeling humbly and meekly before Christ in the next? Reepicheep's passionate yearning for Aslan does not make him weak, nor does his gentlemanly conduct make him soft. On the contrary, his conduct provides him with a strong and secure sense of self, even as his yearning gives his life direction and purpose. Reepicheep knows who he is and where he is going in a way that is unfortunately quite rare in our modern society. Indeed, in chapter 14, as he prepares to leave the island of Ramandu for the unknown dangers of the last and easternmost sea, he proclaims what is my single favorite speech in all the chronicles:

> My own plans are made. While I can, I sail east in the *Dawn Treader*. When she fails me, I paddle east in my coracle. When she sinks, I shall swim east with my four

paws. And when I can swim no longer, if I have not reached Aslan's country, or shot over the edge of the world in some vast cataract, I shall sink with my nose to the sunrise and Peepiceek will be head of the talking mice in Narnia.

We hear a lot today in the media about kids seeking after their dreams, but most of it appeals either (at best) to artificial, cloying sentiment or (at worst) to the child's early stirrings of vanity, greed, and envy. Reepicheep's commitment to achieving his dream has nothing to do with being a pop star or making it rich or getting one over on the snobby kids at school (in fact, Lewis himself strongly disliked children's stories that promised such prizes). What Lewis's chivalrous mouse is after is something far less tangible, something more spiritual than physical. His Holy Grail is not a pot of treasure or a kingdom to rule, but the fulfillment of the very purpose for which he was created. What awaits him at the end of his journey is not celebration but consummation.

If Reepicheep is (at least as I see it) the central hero of *The Voyage of the Dawn Treader*, then who is the chief villain? Oddly, though the novel does boast a particularly seedy bad guy in the person of the corrupt and craven Governor Gumpas, the book finally lacks a White Witch or Miraz to serve as its focal point of evil. Indeed, the real evil in the novel is not so much personal as it is allegorical. As in any good quest romance (and Reepicheep's presence on board forces us to read it in that context), the hero must face not a single antagonist but a series of trials that will test his valor and his purity. Accordingly, Lewis places Reepicheep (and his fellow sailors) in a number of situations that challenge them to overcome such deadly sins as pride, envy, avarice, and sloth (that is why *The Voyage of the Dawn Treader*, for all its narrative thrust, is the most episodic of the Chronicles). In some cases, the crew overcome these challenges by their own resources of strength and virtue, but in most, they escape only because of the miraculous intervention of Aslan, who appears now as a bird to guide them out of danger, now as an imposing presence to shock two of them out of their greed, now as a face in a magic book to prevent another from succumbing to vanity. Even Caspian himself must be rebuked out of his stubborn willfulness through the medium of a golden lion's head on the wall of his cabin.

Indeed, I cannot read through *The Voyage of the Dawn Treader* without a verse from 1 Corinthians popping into my head several times: "There hath no temptation taken you but such as is common to man: but God is faithful, who will not suffer you to be tempted above that ye are able; but will with the temptation also make a way to escape, that ye may be able to bear it" (10:13). Along with *The Horse and His Boy*, *The Voyage of the Dawn Treader* presents its audience (especially its child audience) with a picture of the world that is not far removed from that of *The Divine Comedy*, *Pilgrim's Progress*, or *Canterbury Tales*. In an age when children (and their parents) are continually commanded to live in the now (not in the eschatological now of the kingdom, but the selfish, ephemeral now of immediate gratification), it is good that we be reminded that we are all pilgrims and sojourners in the land. We must be reminded (vis-à-vis the verse quoted above) that what we most need is daily grace to overcome the trials and temptations set before us on the road.

CHAPTER 11:

COURAGE ALONG THE ROAD

B ut how are we to keep on track as we travel that road? To find an answer to that question, we must read on to the next of the chronicles, *The Silver Chair*, a novel that seems at first to be patterned after the very school stories that Lewis hated so much, but that quickly metamorphoses into something far richer and stranger. This time, two children (Eustace and Jill) are called into Narnia by Aslan to help rescue Rilian, the kidnapped son of King Caspian. To help them fulfill their mission, Aslan teaches Jill four Signs that will direct her and Eustace to the missing Prince. He then instructs her to repeat the Signs to herself day and night, taking great care never to forget or overlook them. Broadly speaking, the Signs upon which Jill is instructed to meditate are an allegory for the Bible (Joshua 1:8), or, to be more specific, for those biblical principles and admonitions that Jewish and Christian parents are exhorted to raise their children in (Proverbs 22:6). The remembering or forgetting of these principles does not, in itself, make us good or evil people; however, if we practice the former, we will find ourselves more fit to resist evil and embrace good, while if we succumb to the latter, we will find ourselves an easy prey to all manner of temptation and deception.

Indeed, the choices that Jill and Eustace must make during the course of the novel are inscribed between two poles of good and evil that exert an equally strong pull on the children. These two poles are themselves embodied in two of Lewis's most original creations: the Emerald Witch and Puddleglum. At first glance, the Witch may seem to be merely a stock "bad guy," but, as he did with Miraz, Lewis invests her with an additional sinister quality that delves into the nature of evil itself. For the last ten years, the Emerald Witch has been holding Rilian's body and mind captive in her underground lair. Through her black arts, she has enchanted Rilian into forgetting his true identity and into believing that she is his benefactor. She has further enchanted a race of gnomes into building tunnels for her that will connect her cave with Narnia. When the tunnels are ready, she plans to mount a sneak attack from below on the unsuspecting Narnians and set up Rilian as a puppet King with herself as the true Monarch and Queen. When Eustace and Jill arrive in Narnia, the Emerald Witch is but weeks away from making her attack. Just in time, the children reach the underground cave and rescue Rilian, but, before they can return to the surface, the Witch catches them in the act.

At this point, the reader expects that the Witch will use her powers to kill or at least imprison Rilian and his rescuers, but instead she throws some magic dust in the fire and attempts to enchant them. Slowly, seductively, she convinces our protagonists of a "truth" that they all know is absurd: namely, that neither Narnia nor Aslan exists. There is no outside world with a sun to shine on it (as the children feebly try to convince her); all that exists is her underground cave. That thing which they call the sun is just a dream they made up from staring too long at a torch; all their foolish talk about golden lions is the result of a wish fulfillment spurred on by a yellow cat they once spied in the Witch's chambers. That evil and lies go hand in hand is a fact that few need to be taught—Jesus himself told us that Satan is the Father of Lies; accordingly, Lewis digs further beneath this correlation to uncover the real essence of the satanic lie. The falsehoods of the Witch are more than deceptive; they are nihilistic. For the weak, buffoonish Miraz, it is enough to dismiss the stories of Aslan as old legends with little historical validity; for the far more clever and malevolent Witch, Aslan (and Narnia with him) is to be reduced to nothing but a weak, childish fantasy. The Witch does not seek merely to pervert the truth or alter reality; she wishes to devour them whole. Her final goal is to absorb into herself the personality of the Narnians, as she has already absorbed that of Rilian and the gnomes. Indeed, in a grotesque irony, the Witch arranges for the children (who, having forgotten the Signs, have lost their protection from her lies) to be devoured literally by a race of cannibalistic giants. (Let us not forget that Lewis, in *The Screwtape Letters*, depicts the devils as feasting on the souls of the damned.) It is no coincidence that the Witch, with her underground cave and army of enchanted diggers, strongly resembles a queen ant running a hive. Her evil, totalitarian vision of the perfect state is one in which all citizens are reduced to mindless drones.

It is most fortunate, then, for Eustace, Jill, and Rilian that they have in their company a creature who absolutely cannot be pressed down to fit a generic mold. I refer, of course, to Puddleglum, a Narnian Marshwiggle, whom Lewis once declared was (along with Reepicheep) his favorite character from the Chronicles. Though he is arguably the real hero of *The Silver Chair* (just as Sam is arguably the hero of *The Lord of the Rings*), Puddleglum is more stubborn than Trumpkin and has a streak of pessimism a mile wide and two miles long. He is certainly not your typical follower of Aslan—more like the grouchy guy who sits in the back of the church and grumbles about the pews being too hard than the diplomatic pastor or the charismatic worship leader. And yet, when the moment of decision comes, he is the one who shows the firmest faith in Aslan and the Signs and the greatest willingness to resist the seductive lies of the Witch. He even bravely stamps his foot into the Witch's fire to help clear his head and free the others from the effects of the magic dust. Puddleglum is the perfect embodiment of that old adage that says that you can't judge a book by its cover; that goodness and truth often come in strange and unexpected forms. More than that, he is an object lesson for American children who are taught from the moment they can watch the television that if they want to be good and successful little Americans, they must conform themselves and their dreams to a fixed image—that is to say, they must strive to be "just like everybody else." Despite all the talk of diversity and multiculturalism and alternate lifestyles in our schools, the overwhelming pressure exerted on young Americans is to let themselves be molded by whatever the reigning orthodoxy or fashion happens to be. Puddleglum alone offers incontestable proof that the Chronicles were written not by an American, but by a citizen of a nation that loves and respects its eccentrics; that does not consider egalitarianism some high and holy calling but delights in idiosyncrasy, quixotic behavior, and inefficiency.

Democracy, as far as it goes, is a good thing, but when it begins to run roughshod over personal quirks, when it tries to mold its citizens into a collective mass, it becomes a danger to humanity itself. The trouble with liberalism in America is not that it allows too much variety, but that it allows too little. It would be a very good and healthy thing if every American parent introduced his child to Puddleglum and then used that introduction to drive home one simple rule of thumb: the impulse that would make everyone the same is more often an evil than a good one. The good God who created our universe revels in difference and variety; the enemies of that good God despise all those things that make us unique individuals. There are many religious folk out there who wrongly believe that the satanic ideal for mankind is a Friday night dance hall in New Orleans. It is not so. The Devil, that inveterate hater of our humanity, would like nothing more than to convert our world into a single, giant anthill.

Having provided this dual vision of free humanity vs. mindless conformity in *The Silver Chair*, Lewis goes on in the fifth Chronicle, *The Horse and His Boy*, to follow a group of pilgrims as they seek to move from the latter vision to the former. As before, Lewis provides us with a male and a female protagonist, but this time, neither the boy nor the girl is from our world. The boy, Shasta, is a Prince of Archenland (a good kingdom that lies to the south of Narnia) who was kidnapped while still a baby and who has been raised by a cruel man in the harsh, heathen land of Calormen (which lies south of Archenland). The girl, Aravis, is a spoiled but free-spirited Princess of Calormen, who is pledged by her unloving father to marry the Grand Vizier, a grotesque, toadying, much older man, whom she despises. At the outset of the novel, both Shasta and Aravis (with the help of their talking Narnian horses) decide to escape from Calormen and flee north to Narnia. Though the boy is poor and powerless and the girl is rich and well connected, they yearn alike for a kind of freedom that does not exist in Calormen: a freedom both of body and of spirit. They sense within themselves that they were born for something better, for a world that does not run (as Calormen runs) on treachery, greed, oppression, and slavery.

Like Reepicheep in *The Voyage of the Dawn Treader*, Shasta and Aravis are pilgrims on an allegorical journey—or, to be more precise, an *archetypal* one. An archetype is a person or an object or an event that has universal, cross-cultural significance, a recurring image that surfaces again and again in the myths and legends of diverse groups (water, fire, the quest, and the wise old master are all archetypes). Indeed, of all the characters in The Chronicles of Narnia, Shasta is the most richly archetypal (Prince Caspian is a close second). He is the foundling, the noble (often royal) son who is raised as a peasant, but whose true "blue blood" eventually leads him back to his noble origins; he goes by a hundred names: Percival, Perseus, Hercules, Tarzan, Oliver Twist, Romulus, Cyrus, Moses, Luke Skywalker, Harry Potter. And, of course, Jesus of Nazareth. He is a type, finally, of what we all are: sons and daughters of the King who have been expelled from the garden that was meant to be our home and who are impelled by an inner longing to trudge on, with weary step and slow, to regain that which we have lost. The good that remains within us yearns to be transplanted back into that good soil, for we know that we will never truly be whole until we have returned to our primal place of origin. And that sacred place belongs not just to those who were (like Shasta) actually born there (allegorically and archetypally speaking, Narnia and Archenland are the same place), but to those (like Aravis) whose Narnian birthright is written not in their genes but in their souls.

If you would instill in your children the virtue of pressing on, if you would inspire in them the desire to seek out their purpose no matter the obstacles, then encourage them to identify with Shasta and Aravis. Let them know that those who truly seek with all of their hearts that which is proper for them to know will always find it. Assure them that such seekers will receive divine aid in ways that they could not possibly have imagined or planned for. As in *The Voyage of the Dawn Treader*, Aslan intercedes several times to aid his weary travelers. But this time around, that it *is* Aslan who is helping them is not made clear to them (or to the reader!). Indeed, neither Shasta nor Aravis possesses any real knowledge of Aslan, much less that it is he who is protecting and guiding them. Just so, late converts to Christianity can generally identify (with the help of hindsight) numerous occasions in their pre-Christian walk when the Holy Spirit intervened directly (but "invisibly") in their lives. In that sense, *The Horse and His Boy* is much like the biblical book of Esther, a strange, archetypal book in which God, though he is behind all that happens, is never mentioned by name. God cares, Esther assures us, even for those Jews who have become absorbed into a non-Jewish culture; just so, Aslan watches over all of those who truly desire to do his will, whether they live in Narnia, Archenland, or Calormen.

As *The Horse and His Boy* shares with *The Voyage of the Dawn Treader* its central metaphor of quest/pilgrimage, so does it share as well the narrative device of sending its protagonists through a series of trials. This time, however, Lewis makes it even clearer to his readers that the obstacles his pilgrims must face are as much internal as external. The character flaws in Shasta and Aravis are quickly made evident: the former is selfish, untrusting, and dishonest; the latter is vain, self-centered, and arrogant. They fight often and only learn slowly to trust and respect one another. They both have a host of inner demons and lingering fears that they must overcome if they are to complete their journey. To make it worse, they (and all of Narnia) must protect themselves from an antagonist whose selfishness and vanity are almost boundless: Prince Rabadash of Calormen. Rabadash, more than a simple villain, embodies the archetype of the doppelgänger or ghostly double; he is the evil twin of Shasta/Aravis, an object lesson of what they might themselves have become apart from their yearnings for Narnia and the grace of Aslan. In the manner almost of a parable or a fable, Lewis allows Shasta/Aravis and Rabadash to complete the physical and moral trajectories of their opposing journeys in such a way as to illustrate boldly that we reap what we sow. At the end of the former journey, Shasta and Aravis find freedom, truth, acceptance, and purpose; at the end of the latter, Rabadash forfeits not only his pride and egomania, but his very status as a human being. Thus, while Shasta is restored to his true identity as Prince (and later King) of Archenland, the unrepentant Rabadash is transformed by Aslan into that which he truly is: a donkey. As in *Pinocchio* (another great children's novel filled with teachable moments on the nature of good and evil), either we become consumed by cupidity and make an ass of ourselves, or we seek the selfless road of charity and become, in the end, a real boy.

CHAPTER 12:

THE HEIRS OF NIETZSCHE

O f all the chronicles, *The Magician's Nephew* presents us with the fullest study of the origins, motives, and justifications of evil, a study that, were it presented in philosophical terms, would be above the heads of even teen readers, but that, embodied as it is in the personalities and actions of the tale's two villains, becomes remarkably accessible. *The Magician's Nephew* begins in the early 1900s when two children, Digory and Polly, stumble upon the hidden room of Digory's uncle, Andrew. Andrew is a magician who has in his possession a set of yellow and green rings with the power to transport those who touch them to another world. Andrew desires the forbidden knowledge promised by these other worlds but is too afraid to risk the journey. Unwilling to deny himself the knowledge he seeks, Andrew, without feeling a shred of guilt, manipulates Polly into grabbing one of the rings; whereupon, she vanishes. When Digory rebukes his uncle for behaving dishonestly and for putting Polly into danger, Andrew patiently explains that magicians like himself are above such schoolboy rules of morality and that they are free to use whatever means necessary to further their research. Then, in the same breath, Andrew turns upon

Digory and shames him into taking a ring himself and following Polly into the unknown.

As it turns out, the ring takes him, not to another world, but to a way station, a magical wood dotted with ponds, each of which is a doorway to a different world. Polly and Digory jump into one of the pools and end up in a dead world called Charn. After some exploring, they come upon a great hall filled with statues. Near the statue of a beautiful but cruel-looking woman, they find a bell with an inscription that tempts them to ring the bell. Impulsively, his heart filled with an Andrew-like desire for forbidden knowledge, Digory rings it. Immediately, the statue comes to life, and they learn, to their horror, that she (Queen Jadis) was responsible for the destruction of Charn. After much occult research and personal sacrifice, she had discovered the secret of the "Deplorable Word," a spell she had used to destroy everyone in Charn except herself. When Polly rebukes Jadis for killing innocent people in her quest for power, Jadis responds (undaunted and without a tinge of remorse) that the people of Charn *belonged* to her to do with as she pleased and that, after all, it was her sister's pride that had "forced" her to speak the word. Realizing that Jadis is an evil woman not to be trusted, Polly and Digory try to escape, first to the wood, then back to their world, but both times Jadis grabs hold of them and is pulled in with them. Back in London, Jadis makes Andrew her apprentice-slave and sets out to take over the city. In desperation, Polly and Digory use their rings to spirit her away, but, by accident, also drag in Andrew, a cabby (Frank), and his horse (Strawberry). The rings, however, end up carrying them not back to Charn but to a new world about to be born.

That world, of course, is Narnia, and as the six travelers watch in wonder, Aslan sings Narnia into being. Digory, Polly, Frank, and Strawberry are captivated by the song, but Jadis and Andrew, whose hearts are insensitive to love and joy, hate the sound. So deep is their hatred, in fact, that Jadis takes a piece of a lamppost she had ripped off in London for a weapon and throws it at Aslan's forehead. It bounces off harmlessly and falls to the ground, where, miraculously, it grows into a lamppost. As the others marvel at the fertility of Narnia's new soil, Andrew thinks only of the weapons he could grow: he would turn paradise into a munitions factory! That which inspires awe and praise in the others inspires only fear, greed, and loathing in the twisted souls of Andrew and Jadis.

Much more happens in the novel (indeed, *The Magician's Nephew* is, to my mind at least, the most tightly and effectively plotted of all the chronicles), but, for the purposes of this chapter, we may stop here. I do not mince words when I say that if parents could successfully convey to their children the exact nature of the evil that impels Andrew and Jadis, they would have gone a long way toward shielding their progeny from a kind of madness and deception that has destroyed individuals and whole societies throughout recorded history. This particular form of self-delusion is first described (and exposed) in Plato's *Republic*, that great dialogue which attempts the vital task of defining justice. One of the characters in the dialogue, whose views Plato most strongly critiques, is a man named Thrasymachus. According to him, justice is nothing more than the will of the stronger: might makes right. The victors not only reap the spoils and write the history books but also determine what is or is not just. Two millennia later, at the dawn of the Renaissance, Machiavelli would echo Thrasymachus's definition in his own anti-Platonic meditation on justice and the state: *The Prince*. Rejecting what he saw as the idealistic and impractical position taken by Plato, Machiavelli argued that in our world, expediency always wins out: the ends justify the means. The wise ruler is one who can appear to be virtuous while practicing every from of deceit necessary to achieve his ends.

Another four hundred years would go by before Thrasymachus and Machiavelli would find an even more radical disciple who would question the very status of virtue and vice, a philosopher who would urge his ideal leader, his man of the future, to move himself beyond all bourgeois notions of good and evil. That philosopher was Nietzsche, and he dubbed his messianic leader the Overman. Morality, culture, and the state had all grown petty and corrupt for Nietzsche; modern religion was but a sham, a slave ethic used by the weak to keep the powerful in check. What was needed was not a revival of the Platonic or (worse yet) Christian notion of justice; what was needed was a strong leader who was unafraid to tear down old institutions and ideologies, a leader who possessed what Nietzsche called a "will to power." Fast-forward one more century, and we come to the logically illogical end of Thrasymachus's argument that might makes right. In the work of the postmodern historian and theorist Michel Foucault, we learn that society and humanity are defined not by virtues like justice, honor, or love, but by structures of power. In fact, it is those structures (and those structures alone) that produce and define our notions of justice, honor, and love: no one can think outside of the structure. For Foucault, might *literally* makes right; the Platonic or Christian notion of justice is just one of many possible ideologies determined by the reigning regime of power.

Try to explain the last two paragraphs to your ten-year-old, and you won't get very far. But introduce him to Andrew and Jadis, and he will not only see the seed of Thrasymachus in action but also see the bitter fruit that grows from such seeds. Indeed, Digory himself sees almost immediately through the self-serving hypocrisy of Andrew (and, behind him, Thrasymachus and his heirs). Andrew, like all of his ilk, considers himself superior to standard rules of morality (beyond good and evil); yet, he simultaneously expects Digory to heed the call of honor and rescue Polly. As for Jadis, Polly sees just as clearly through her façade. If Jadis is so convinced that her actions are above the reproach of middle-class morality, if she is so assured of the purity of her will to power, then why does she feel the need to justify her actions by blaming her sister for the destruction of Charn? Jadis and Andrew stand accused by their own words, but they are so thoroughly narcissistic that they cannot see it. Their Faustian lust for knowledge and power is so boundless, so unquenchable, that they are willing to surrender their own capacity for true happiness and joy in exchange. Those who champion the ideals of Nietzsche generally consider themselves to be pragmatic, clear-thinking people whose eyes have been opened to the delusions of those trapped in a "limited" Judeo-Christian mindset. And yet, ironically, such people often end up (like Andrew and Jadis) blind to the greater realities that lie all around them. Like the Pharisees who witnessed Jesus' miracles with their own eyes yet were unable to recognize his glory, so Andrew and Jadis are utterly blind to the beauty and wonder of Narnia. In the presence of a fellow Israelite cured of leprosy, the Pharisees can see only the legal infraction (Jesus healed on the Sabbath); in the presence of the unbounded fertility of Narnia, Uncle Andrew sees only the potential to create weapons of mass destruction.

"There is a way," Proverbs warns us, "which seemeth right unto a man, but the end thereof are the ways of death" (14:12). The way of Thrasymachus, of Machiavelli, of Nietzsche, of Foucault (like the way of Andrew and Jadis) may seem at first to be enlightened, fashionable, and "brave," but it leads in the end to death.

Thematically speaking, *The Magician's Nephew* is a complex book, and, as such, it prepares the way for an even *more* complex book: *The Last Battle*. (The dual complexity of these two books offers yet another reason why they should be read in their proper order, as the final two chronicles of the series.) Here, in the most apocalyptic of the tales, Lewis presents us with a trio of Nietzsche-like villains whose cumulative treachery ushers in the end of Narnia. It all begins when a Machiavellian ape named Shift convinces his "friend" (a naive donkey appropriately named Puzzle) to dress up in a lion skin and pretend to be Aslan. The dialogue that Lewis writes for Shift and Puzzle is simple but remarkably effective; even a child can see through the loathsome tricks Shift uses to bend Puzzle to his will while simultaneously understanding how Puzzle could be so easily fooled. Shift used a combination of guilt and false piety to achieve his ends. Although his motives are purely selfish and self-aggrandizing, he pretends that his real goal is to help Puzzle and the rest of Narnia reach their full potential. With a broad, rhetorical flourish, he casts himself in the role of noble sufferer, of one who has (to paraphrase Andrew and Jadis) a high and lonely destiny to fulfill. Like Andrew and Jadis (or, for that matter, like Satan), he mounts a great lie and then comes to believe it himself. While spouting promises of modern efficiency and collective prosperity for Narnia (all in the name of the false Aslan he has erected), he scourges the land for profit and sells the talking beasts into slavery in Calormen. He even dons human clothing and deludes his followers (and perhaps *himself*) into believing that he is not, in fact, an ape, but a very old and wrinkled man.

Into this moral and spiritual vacuum, a second, more effective Overman (Rishda Tarkaan) soon enters and supplants the petty visions of empire dreamed up by Shift (who is even more buffoonish than Uncle Miraz). A combination of Hitler, Stalin, Mussolini, and every other twentieth-century totalitarian despot, Rishda is a Calormen general whose avaricious will to power surpasses even that of Rabadash. With the help of his "propaganda minister" (a talking cat named Ginger), he extends and complicates Shift's deceptions by claiming that Aslan and the idolatrous, vulture-headed god of Calormen (Tash) are actually the same god. In the name of this new god (Tashlan), Rishda destroys what is left of Narnian freedom and poisons what little faith, hope, and love remain. In fact, so thoroughly does he corrupt the wellsprings of Narnia's religion that when Puzzle is exposed as a false Aslan, the Narnians do not return to worshiping the real Aslan but give in to utter apathy and despair. As in *The Magician's Nephew*, Lewis's warning here draws on concepts from philosophy, sociology, and political science that would normally be beyond the comprehension of child readers. And yet, once again, Lewis makes the academic and arcane both accessible and urgent. The Bible tells us that Satan often disguises himself as an angel of light; similarly, evil in our world often cloaks itself in fine-sounding words like *tolerance, egalitarianism*, and *patriotism*. Rather than reason abstractly, *The Last Battle* demonstrates how swiftly relativism can lead to nihilism, the free market to oppression, progress to dehumanization, and promises of utopia into the harsh realities of dystopia.

Of course, a number of "good guys" rise up to defend Narnia from the evil of Shift, Rishda, and Ginger: Tirian (the last King of Narnia), Jewel (a noble unicorn), Roonwit (a wise centaur), Poggin the dwarf (who refuses to cave in to the cynicism and "ethnocentrism" of his fellow dwarfs), and Eustace and Jill (who have been called back into Narnia by the righteous prayers of Tirian). Together, these heroes and their loyal followers mount a brave offensive again the "bad guys" and . . . lose! In sharp contrast to the other six chronicles, the heroes of *The Last Battle* are all defeated by the forces of evil. Though this ending is, in some ways, forced on Lewis by the apocalyptic nature of the tale, he goes out of his way to emphasize the eventual defeat of Tirian's rebels and the destruction of Narnia. That nothing on our Earth lasts forever, that all things must come to an end, was a message Lewis hoped (I believe) to impress on our death-denying age. If there is one thing that modern American parents and schools do not teach their young charges, it is the fact that all in our world will eventually die and decay. This may sound like a contradictory statement given Pope John Paul II's perceptive observation that Western society has embraced a culture of death, but it is less contradictory than it is paradoxical. Our society's simultaneous acceptance of abortion and euthanasia and its false promise that we can live forever in perfect health are but two symptoms, I would argue, of the same disease: an inability and an unwillingness to accept the natural risks that accompany life in a fallen world (the excessive amount of litigation in our country may also be traced back to this same disease). We, like Tirian, want to be in control of ourselves and our surroundings; we find it impossible to believe that hard work and commitment will not lead to success and happiness. Of course, in most cases, they do, but not always. Oftentimes, there is no way to avoid defeat, overcome disease, and cheat death; the true hero knows this, and, though he will fight bravely while there is still a chance of victory, he knows too how to accept that which cannot be avoided.

There is a rumor out there that evil is realistic, pragmatic, and savvy while goodness is idealistic, gullible, and naive. It is not so. Evil always deceives, and, in the end, that deceit blinds even itself. It is the good whose eyes are truly opened to the real, the lasting, and the true. It is goodness that stares reality in the face and accepts—accepts, but never resigns. For the Chronicles begin and end with a death that leads to a resurrection. In the first chronicle, that death is limited to Aslan; in the last, the heroic champions of Aslan share in their Master's death.

In his epistle to the church at Philippi, Paul longs that he may know Christ "and the power of his resurrection, and the fellowship of his sufferings, being made conformable unto his death; if by any means I might attain unto the resurrection of the dead" (3:10–11). Tirian and his men are at their most heroic, their most "Aslan-like," not when they are killing Calormenes, but when they willingly take onto themselves the fellowship of Aslan's sufferings on the Stone Table. This statement alone might suggest a kind of defeatism or martyr complex in Lewis's heroes, but then the statement is not to be taken alone. Though Lewis loved Norse mythology and was a devotee of Wagner's Ring cycle, he understood that the dark Teutonic fascination with violent death and self-immolation was not, finally, compatible with the Christian focus on the crucifixion. Yes, it is right that Christian (and Narnian) martyrs should long to participate in the fellowship of his (Christ's/Aslan's) suffering, but only so that they might share as well in his resurrection. Though the second half of *The Last Battle* may seem to give us Lewis at his most pessimistic and Germanic, the death and defeat through which the characters must suffer prove less a capitulation to the Teutonic fascination with death than a prelude to Christian glory and apotheosis. The concluding chapters of the novel offer a depiction of heaven that combines Plato, Revelation, and Dante in a heady, imaginative mixture that remains in the mind (of child and adult alike) long after the book has been completed and laid back on the shelf.

Yes, the Chronicles of Narnia offer us a glorious happy ending (replete with a joyous "cast party" that reunites all the characters from the previous six tales), but it is an ending that has been hard fought and even harder won. In the end, good does not simply defeat evil; good and evil become, at last, what they truly are. Evil is confined to darkness, not so much out of retributive justice but because evil never truly embraced or desired the light. Goodness, on the other hand, opens out onto eternal light and boundless space for that was what *it* ever yearned for while it struggled and groaned for consummation.

This is something that every true hero knows and longs for in his heart and that no true villain can ever, ever hope to understand.

MEN WITHOUT CHESTS

CHAPTER 13:

LOSING THE TAO

S ince the disturbing photos of tortured Iraqi prisoners hit television screens across the country in the spring of 2004, a national dialogue has raged as to how American soldiers could engage in such brutal and unethical behavior. Many were shocked that "nice American boys and girls" could be capable of such vicious acts and asked, in one form or another, that age-old question: "Hasn't anyone ever taught these kids right from wrong?" The answer I'm afraid has become, increasingly, "no."

Of course, that such is the state of affairs in America (not to mention Europe and Canada) should come as no surprise to anyone who has read what is surely C. S. Lewis's most prophetic work: *The Abolition of Man* (1943). For you see, though modern public education in the West has not fully abandoned the concept of ethics and morality, it has quite clearly abandoned what C. S. Lewis dubbed the "Tao." According to Lewis, the Tao (as defined in chapters 1 and 2 of *The Abolition of Man* as well as in book I of *Mere Christianity*) is the universal moral law code known and understood by all peoples at all times and across all cultures. The Tao is not a man-made product but is given by God and is apprehended by all people through natural reason (i.e., through the conscience that all men possess by virtue of being created in the image of God) and through revelation (divinely given law codes like the Ten Commandments and the Sermon on the Mount). On this ethical (as opposed to theological) level, all religions and cultures are more or less at one with Christianity. Indeed, so central has the Tao been to our conception of ourselves as human beings, that it has always played a central role in one of humanity's most vital and enduring tasks: the education of the young.

Unfortunately for the youth of modern America (and we adults who must live with the decisions those youths will make when they themselves become adults), the real presence of a universal moral code that is older than man and that rests finally on revelation is a concept that has been dismissed—indeed, expelled—from public education. This rejection of a type of education that lies at the core of our Greco-Roman and Judeo-Christian heritage has been justified on at least three grounds: "scientific" (modern education is to rest on logic, reason, and empirical evidence, not on divine revelation), sociological-anthropological (what we in the West call morality is not universal but culture specific), and political (a "religious" concept like the Tao has no place in public, state-run education). Of course, by so doing, the educational system has courted disaster. When the government removed the Bible from the public classroom in the 1960s, it also removed all standards and touchstones against which teachers and students alike could measure their beliefs and actions. If a precocious *or* belligerent third grader were to ask his teacher why it is wrong to steal another boy's lunch but his teacher were prevented by law from appealing to the Ten Commandments (that is, to the Tao), then the teacher could finally offer only one answer: because I say so (that is to say, because I'm stronger and have authority).

Not so, the critic will immediately answer. Could not the teacher explain to the boy that he has a duty to society and to his fellow man not to take what does not belong to him? Could she not reason with the boy (as Kant would) that if all boys stole what they wanted, the result would be chaos? Could she not appeal to his sense of honor and fair play or perhaps ask him to put himself in the shoes of the boy he wants to steal from? The answer, finally, is no. To offer any of these answers, the teacher must appeal to that very Tao which has been considered "out of bounds" by the makers of our modern (and postmodern) society. In the absence of the Tao, who is to say that duty means anything more than serving your own interests or that social order and stability are "good" (as opposed to "bad") things that ought to be preserved. Indeed, to use the word "ought" at all presupposes a standard (the Tao) that *all* should follow, whether young or old, student or teacher, weak or powerful. Modern educators (and public servants in general) are prone to make statements like the following: "This drug will save lives; therefore, it should be immediately approved by the FDA." What they often fail to realize is that such statements (what logicians call enthymemes) cannot be made unless we first accept a major premise or assumption: in this case, that human lives are of intrinsic value and are thus worth saving at all costs. This premise, however, is intrinsically linked to the Tao; it is an assumption that we do not argue *for* but *from*. Unless it and other such premises are accepted first (a priori), neither logical thought nor judgments of value can follow.

Very well, says the critic, such grand appeals to duty and societal order are perhaps a bit out of date. What the teacher really needs to do is simply to explain that honesty is a virtue and stealing is a vice. But this approach, too, leads to a dead end. On the simplest level, the appeal to virtue/vice won't work, since one cannot distinguish between the two unless one has a touchstone to measure them against (without the Tao, virtue is inevitably reduced to the will of the stronger: might makes right). On a deeper level, however, the appeal to virtue (and to values in general) is destroyed by the very pedagogical approach taken in the modern classroom. As Lewis demonstrates in his analysis of *The Green Book* in chapter 1 of *The Abolition of Man*, modern (which is to say, post-Enlightenment) education instills in its young charges the belief that all value judgments are finally subjective. When we say that something is beautiful or ugly, sublime or ordinary, we are not saying anything concrete about the object in question. We are saying, rather, that our *response* to that object seems to make it beautiful, ugly, sublime, or ordinary.

Though Lewis does not trace the origin of this (epistemological) method of perceiving and judging the world around us, it can be traced back to two seminal works: Edmund Burke's *A Philosophical Inquiry into the Origin of Our Ideas of the Sublime and the Beautiful* (1757) and Immanuel Kant's *Critique of Judgment* (1790). Both Burke and Kant make a vital distinction between the subject (a conscious self that perceives) and the object (an unconscious thing that does not perceive but is, rather, perceived by a subject). When Burke and Kant label our response to art as purely subjective, they mean that the experience has nothing to do with the object per se (whether it be a poem, a painting, or a song), but exists wholly in the mind of the subject: it is not the flower itself that is beautiful, but the feelings that exist in the mind of the person who is looking at the flower. Still, though Burke and Kant insisted that our response to such things as beauty and sublimity is totally subjective, they firmly believed that our subjective response had universal validity: that everyone should and must feel about it in the same way. Neither philosopher, that is to say, was a modern relativist; yet, ironically, tragically, their "subjectivizing" of the arts opened a Pandora's box that led the way directly to modern relativism. For, if beauty lies truly (and only) in the eye of the beholder, if things really exist only inasmuch as they are perceived, then ultimately there can be no higher standard against which our responses to art can be measured.

———

In the above paragraph, I focused on the arts, but the subjective approach initiated by Burke and Kant (it is foreshadowed as far back as Descartes) eventually found its way into all statements of value, including those having to do with virtue and vice. One of the unfortunate legacies of the Enlightenment (whose central figure was none other than Kant) was to initiate a radical split between the head and the heart, the rational and the emotional, the logical and the intuitive. Over the last two hundred years, it has become increasingly the norm in the West to make a firm divide between facts on the one hand (the natural and social sciences) and values on the other (religion, ethics, and the humanities). Only in the former category are we to encounter objective truths on which to ground society. The (wholly subjective) truths that arise out of the latter category are fine for individual edification and enrichment, but they cannot serve as the basis of social institutions, government policy, or state-run education. One might be able to calculate scientifically the percentage of soldiers who will run away or stay their ground in a given battle, but to start speaking of courage and cowardice, honor and dishonor as if they were real, objective things that can be measured is to try to turn mere values into concrete facts. The coldly logical man who treats his wife's yearnings for attention as merely emotional outbursts does not necessarily dismiss her yearnings as nonexistent; he simply refuses to ascribe to them any rational or objective validity. Modern education, I'm afraid, often treats traditional, Tao-based virtues in the same way: as merely personal choices that cannot be granted the universal status given to, say, the numerical value of pi, or the scientific theory of evolution, or the economic laws of supply and demand.

And this is a problem—one that threatens to rob education of one of its most traditional and most vital roles in the life of the individual and of the society those individuals are a part of. In the closing paragraphs of chapter 1, Lewis, borrowing a metaphor from Plato, argues that in all human beings there exists a perpetual war between the head (reason) and the belly (appetite). Though it is through the head that we are drawn up toward the angels and through the belly that we are drawn down toward the beasts, in a straight fight between the two, the belly will win every time. Luckily, however, the head is aided by the intervention of the chest, which, Lewis tells us (after Alanus) is the seat "of Magnanimity, of emotions organized by trained habit into stable sentiments." Lewis then concludes: "The Chest—Magnanimity—Sentiment—these are the indispensable liaison officers between cerebral man and visceral man. It may even be said that it is by this middle element that man is man: for by his intellect he is mere spirit and by his appetite mere animal." Without the Tao, therefore, we not only leave the head easy prey to the belly but also cease to be human beings at all. Unfortunately, modern education, by debunking the real, objective status of all Tao-based (as opposed to man-made, culture-specific) virtues and values causes the chest to shrivel.

For the traditional teacher who has not accepted the Enlightenment split of facts and values, it is not enough to teach young students merely knowledge of the Tao. In addition to learning how to distinguish virtuous behavior from vicious behavior, the student must be taught how he is to *feel* about virtue and vice. The student must be trained from a young age to feel good about himself when he performs a virtuous action and to feel a sense of internal disgust (but not of self-hatred) when he does something vicious. When his teacher (or parent) tells him he has been responsible or courageous or honest, his chest should swell and his face light up; when the same teacher (or parent) tells him he has been irresponsible or cowardly or dishonest, he should hang his head and feel a flush of embarrassment in his cheeks. This may sound at first like Pavlovian behaviorism, but it is not. As fallen creatures to whom sin, pride, and disobedience come as naturally as ethics and morality, it is proper and necessary that our emotions be trained along with our minds and souls. By such means is the chest strengthened and expanded.

But modern education, alas, takes the opposite approach. Rather than instill virtue (and its concomitant emotions) in its students, it far too often dismisses and even ridicules such traditional virtues as chastity, patriotism, and honor. Indeed, in American schools, there seem to be only three virtues that are taught with any regularity: environmentalism, tolerance, and egalitarianism. These are fine as far as they go, but the modern educator is too often willing to break all other Tao-based virtues in order to achieve one or all of these treasured three. Thus, in the name of environmentalism, the value of human life is cheapened; in the name of tolerance, sexual morality is discarded; in the name of egalitarianism, virtues like courage, self-control, and wisdom are flattened out to a lowest-common-denominator standard that all can achieve equally. Lest any voices or forms of self-expression be stifled, all traditional standards of beauty are debunked; in order that those lacking imagination not be made to feel any lesser, such emotions as wonder, awe, and reverence are consistently deflated.

And all the while, as our public schools debunk and deflate, society continues to complain that our young people lack a sense of beauty and wonder. "You can hardly open a periodical," writes Lewis in the last paragraph of chapter 1, "without coming across the statement that what our civilization needs is more 'drive,' or dynamism, or self-sacrifice, or 'creativity.' In a sort of ghastly simplicity we remove the organ and demand the function. We make men without chests and expect of them virtue and enterprise. We laugh at honour and are shocked to find traitors in our midst. We castrate and bid the geldings be fruitful." With a mania that would be comical if it were not so potentially destructive, the makers of public education seem intent on removing from the school system every shred of Tao-based (that is to say, Bible-based) morality. By so doing, they think to usher in an educational utopia. Of course, if they were to succeed in achieving their goals and to truly establish a values-free education, they would see that they had sown the seeds of their own destruction. That they had created men without chests. That they had produced precisely the kind of people who could torture and humiliate prisoners without feeling any sense of guilt or remorse.

CHAPTER 14:

THE DANGERS OF A VALUES-FREE EDUCATION

W as C. S. Lewis the first writer to note the link between Tao-less, chest-less education and the producing of young people with no inner sense of moral discernment? He most certainly was not. Indeed, if we are to gain a wider perspective on the dangers posed by modern values-free education, then we must reclaim (and *pay attention to*) those other voices from the past that have warned us of these dangers. In pursuit of this wider perspective, I would like to look briefly at three great works of literature from the classical, medieval, and post-Enlightenment eras that testify alike to what happens when we cut ourselves loose from the Tao and allow the chest to shrivel. In the process, I shall consider three distinct manifestations of a Tao-less, values-free education that threatens to produce a generation of young people who will eventually turn against those who thought to liberate and expand their minds: (1) the systematic killing of all imagination in the name of reason and logic; (2) the all-out rejection of the Tao and the acceptance of pure ethical relativism; and (3) the loss of that vital feeling of disgust that should and must accompany breaches of the Tao.

The first manifestation is a uniquely modern one that rises up out of that Enlightenment split between the rational and the emotional discussed above. Flush with the utilitarian theories of Jeremy Bentham and James Mill, nineteenth-century England rushed headlong into a new educational initiative that would ground itself on facts, logic, and empiricism and would eschew all arts, all imagination, and all those things that smack of the emotional, the intuitive, or the spiritual. Students were not to waste their time building idealistic castles in the air or pondering religious mysteries about which nothing definite or concrete could be known (the legacy here of David Hume). To the contrary, they were to receive an education that would train them to live in a modern, scientific, technological age. No need to bother about virtuous sentiments or ancient tales of heroes and heroines. Best to keep one's feet on the ground and one's head out of the clouds. Never mind the fact that scientific theories change constantly while the Bible and the *Iliad* are as true today as when they were written. Never mind that children need guidance in judging what is right and wrong, wise and foolish, just and unjust. Just teach them to think in a logical, clearheaded fashion, and everything else will take care of itself.

Charles Dickens was well aware of this post-Enlightenment ethic and to a certain extent shared his era's dreams of building a utopia and bringing order and reason to the globe. But he saw as well the danger in an educational system that allows the chest to atrophy and that kills all stirrings of the imagination. In a fit of prophetic passion not far removed from that which drove Lewis to write *The Abolition of Man*, Dickens produced a short novel that was really a parable in disguise. The novel is titled *Hard Times* (1845), and it tells the unsettling tale of a modern, well-intentioned father (Thomas Gradgrind) who, by educating his children in a Tao-less vacuum that exalts facts above all else, produces a pair of human monsters. Totally unschooled in the affairs of the heart and of the proper feelings associated with love and marriage, his daughter (Louisa) first marries an aged, "filthy-capitalist" banker whom she does not love and who crushes what little spirit she has and then, overpowered by passions she cannot understand, nearly runs off with an amoral rake who would have used and abandoned her. She ends up an empty shell of a woman, a living indictment of her father's faulty theories of education. Gradgrind's son (Tom), on the other hand, bereft of any internal sense of moral and ethical behavior, becomes a thief and a scoundrel who frames an innocent and godly worker and then justifies his crimes to his father in the name of the scientific, utilitarian "values" he had been taught. As if to drive home the cause-effect theme of his novel (namely, that if we create men without chests they will be incapable of virtue, honor, and love), Dickens titles the three sections of his novel Sowing, Reaping, and Garnering.

Dickens, however, goes much further than merely tracing the negative upshot of an empirical-grounded, fact-instilling (rather than a Tao-based, virtue-nurturing) educational system. Through a clever and subtle biblical allusion, he points his reader toward a truth about proper education in the Tao that Lewis would certainly agree with. Book I, chapter 1 of *Hard Times*, which begins with the sentence, "Now, what I want is Facts," and then goes on to lay out the necessity for all learning to stick closely to and never deviate from empirical data, is titled "The One Thing Needful." Book III, chapter 1, in which the distraught Louisa is discovered in an insensible heap before the door of her father and Mr. Gradgrind is forced to ask himself what went wrong, is titled "Another Thing Needful." The two chapter titles allude to a passage from the Gospels:

> Now it came to pass, as they went, that he [Jesus] entered into a certain village: and a certain woman named Martha received him into her house. And she had a sister called Mary, which also sat at Jesus' feet, and heard his word. But Martha was cumbered about much serving, and came to him, and said, Lord, dost thou not care that my sister hath left me to serve alone? Bid her therefore that she help me. And Jesus answered and said unto her, Martha, Martha, thou art careful and troubled about many things: But one thing is needful: and Mary hath chosen that good part, which shall not be taken away from her. (Luke 10:38–42)

A proper schooling in the Tao calls for not only the instilling of virtues, but also the right ordering of those virtues. Gradgrind's modern, "scientific" education has left out the most vital part, the part that makes us most human and that brings us most joy. The things taught in his utilitarian classroom are all things that can be taken away; that which is most lasting and valuable is simply ignored. Such a focusing on the temporal and fleeting at the expense of the durable and perennial is seen in our own modern schools, not only when the fashionable virtues of tolerance, egalitarianism, and environmentalism are raised above the more seminal virtues of courage, wisdom, justice, and self-control, but also when contemporary, "politically correct" texts are chosen over the timeless classics of the Western canon.

Unfortunately, the would-be restorer of the Tao to our modern educational system must contend with far more than this devaluing of imagination, sentiment, and the classical virtues. The anti-Tao stance of modern Western education also manifests itself in a simple dismissal of all set standards or touchstones. Most people consider this impulse to embrace pure subjectivism and relativism to be a recent product of postmodern thought. It is, in fact, a very old impulse that can be traced back to the fifth-century BC sophists against whom Socrates and Plato sought to define themselves. These ancient, "pre-postmodern" philosophers were really itinerant teachers who, for a price, would teach their pupils the arts of rhetoric and logic by which they could learn to make the weaker argument the stronger. (They were also, incidentally, the first cultural and ethical relativists, who taught that morality shifted from one Greek polis to the next and was therefore neither universal nor cross-cultural.) The great Greek comic playwright Aristophanes was an archenemy of the sophists and saw full well the danger posed to the polis (city-state) by their educational theories and practices. Though often considered a "liberal" for the bawdy nature of most of his plays, Aristophanes was, in matter of fact, a reactionary who hoped to return Athens to her more traditional virtues and values (as Cato and Cicero sought to do in the latter days of the Roman Republic). Indeed, in a cogent parallel to modern America, where many wonder if we will ever revive in our young people those strengths and values that empowered us to fight off the twin evils of fascism and communism, Aristophanes hailed the traditional virtues of Athens as the key source of power that enabled her to resist Persian aggression (at the Battle of Marathon in particular) and thus preserve freedom in the West.

In order to illustrate the dangers of a sophistical, values-free education and to show (like Dickens after him) that we reap what we sow, Aristophanes wrote a brilliant comedy that is as parable-like in its form as *Hard Times*. In the play (*Clouds*) a father (Strepsiades) with grand designs for his progeny sends his son (Pheidippides) to the school of the sophists to learn how to make the weaker argument the stronger. His reasons for doing so are purely practical. Strepsiades is in debt, and he wishes to find a way to relieve himself of the burden of paying off his creditors. At first he goes himself to the school of the sophists but is too old and slow-witted to learn their wisdom. Having failed himself, he manages, with much effort, to persuade Pheidippides to go in his place. The son agrees, and, in the second half of the play, Strepsiades does manage to get his debts canceled by making use of the relativistic logic of sophistry.

Unfortunately for the triumphant father, the play does not end here. In the closing scene, Strepsiades and his son get into a debate, and Pheidippides strikes his father. When Strepsiades balks at this treatment and appeals to his son to heed the laws of the polis and of piety, Pheidippides uses his newly learned "logic" to show his father why he is, in fact, committing a proper action in beating (literally) his own father. Repeating what both he and Strepsiades had learned from the sophists, Pheidippides argues that the laws of the state are merely man-made and can therefore be changed and that, as far as piety goes, there really is no such person as Zeus. In many ways *Clouds*, like *Hard Times*, dramatizes a type of argumentative method (used most brilliantly by Jonathan Swift in his essay, "A Modest Proposal") that is still known by its Latin name: reductio ad absurdum. In order to expose the inherent weaknesses in and dangers of an education that either ignores imagination and sentiment or throws out all standards, Dickens and Aristophanes extrapolate outward, to its logically illogical conclusion, such an educational system: in both cases, the creation of a human being with no sense of piety, ethics, or proper behavior. The lesson enshrined in both novel and play is a sobering one: be careful what values you instill in the young; your educational choices may come back to haunt you.

———————

Hard Times and *Clouds* both focus specifically on schools that educate their young charges in a faulty and finally destructive pedagogy. I would like to turn now to one final manifestation of a Tao-less, values-free education that, though it is not presented in terms of an actual school, exposes powerfully what awaits a society that not only debunks the Tao but also fails to instill in its youth the proper feelings that we should associate with virtuous and vicious behavior. I take my case study from the thirtieth canto of Dante's *Inferno*; in this truly gruesome canto, Virgil and Dante make their way through the final *bolgia* (or pit) of level eight, which houses for eternity the falsifiers (opera lovers will be sad to discover Gianni Schicchi among this crew). Here they meet Sinon (who deceived the Trojans into accepting the Wooden Horse) and Master Adam (a notorious counterfeiter of Dante's day). As Dante looks on, Sinon and Master Adam become embroiled in a nasty debate. The two sinners hurl insults and abuses at each other, slandering their opponent even as they justify themselves. Neither feels any shame as they recount the indecencies of their crimes and punishments. Dante slowly becomes mesmerized by their petty quarrel and hangs on their every word. Finally, when he realizes that Dante will continue to listen unless he is aroused, Virgil scolds him sharply and tells him that his desire to listen to such base and unedifying speech is itself degrading. Dante immediately blushes and asks forgiveness, and Virgil tells him that the very shame he feels is sufficient to erase his shame.

Dante's temptation to stay and listen to Sinon and Master Adam may seem remote from twenty-first century America, but most Americans are tempted in the same way several times a week. Be honest! Have you never been surfing through the channels on your television only to come across a daytime talk show (*Jerry Springer, Jenny Jones*, etc.) in which a group of people on stage is sharing with the audience behaviors and actions that most "normal" Americans would never dream of confessing to their own friends? You immediately roll your eyes and exclaim how terrible these shows are and how they are corrupting all who watch them. But when you go to change the channel on the remote control, your finger does not move. You watch for several more minutes and then begin to question the air around you as to why there are so many shows like this on TV and who the poor pathetic people are who actually watch them. And again, you go to change the channel, but your finger does not move. In the end, you watch the entire show, drawn in by its pseudoconfessional nature (pseudo because none of those who deliver the "confessions" feel any remorse or sense of shame) and by the same illicit thrill one gets when one overhears a juicy piece of gossip.

Surely there is nothing wrong with watching such shows, protests the typical American, but there is: the same danger that Virgil warns Dante of. To listen, to absorb, perhaps to enjoy such petty and degrading speech is to dull and finally suspend what has come to be known as our "sense of outrage" (that is to say, that sense of disgust we *should* feel when the Tao is violated). Indeed, even more corrupting than the "confessions" themselves is the behavior of the crowd, the majority of whom actually applaud those who share their immoral, antivirtuous antics. Too often today, public education invites its pupils to witness, like Dante, the Jerry Springer Show of Hell. Before the impressionable eyes and ears of children and teens, classical virtues are dismissed, scorned, and even ridiculed, all in the name of tolerance, egalitarianism, and (God preserve us) the separation of church and state. *Well, that's just human nature,* we are trained to think; *there's nothing really wrong with it, and it's not something that we should really feel ashamed about.* But, of course, that is the very problem. We *should* feel ashamed.

We are told constantly that today's teens are wilder than those of the 1950s, but that is not really true. Young people have always, to a certain extent, been wild. What is different about members of the current generation is not that they do bad things, but that when they do them, they feel no internal sense of guilt or remorse. The '50s boy who had sex outside of marriage would generally feel a twinge of guilt after his action; this twinge would not necessarily prevent him from doing it again, but it at least left open the possibility of true repentance, confession, and regeneration. But today, more and more, the teen performs his rebellious and sinful acts in a guiltless void. As terrifying as were the actual killings that took place at Columbine High School in the 1990s, even more unsettling was what appeared to be a complete lack of remorse or sense of shame in the perpetrators of the deed. In such cases, the chest has not only shriveled; it has completely disappeared. Virtuous sentiment has been swallowed up, and the shells of human beings that remain are left without any moral compass to guide them or ethical boundaries to protect them.

Lewis, I believe, saw all these dangers, but he also knew that they would take several generations to fully manifest themselves. Society may break away from (and ridicule) the Tao, but as long as the young of that society have the Tao (and the proper feelings associated with it) instilled in them by parents and teachers, they will generally return to the Tao, even after a period of rebellion and antisocial behavior (as occurred in our country in the late '60s and early '70s). But if those children grow up and raise *their* children without the Tao, and those children in turn raise their *own* children without the Tao, then will society begin to be plagued by a generation that acts without remorse in a Tao-less vacuum. "I had sooner play cards," writes Lewis in chapter 1 of *The Abolition of Man*, "against a man who was quite sceptical about ethics, but bred to believe that a 'gentleman does not cheat,' than against an irreproachable moral philosopher who had been brought up among sharpers."

"Train up a child in the way he should go," Proverbs 22 tells us, "and when he is old, he will not depart from it." Unfortunately, this well-worn apothegm works in negative as well: train up a child without any set moral parameters, and when he is old, he will depart from morality altogether. Perhaps those "nice" American soldiers who tortured Iraqi prisoners (like those "nice" businessmen whose unethical practices led to the debacles of Enron and other corporations at the turn of the twenty-first century) are the firstfruits of a society that has cut itself loose from the Tao. As has oft been noted, America (and, even more, Europe) is living, quite precariously, on the moral capital built up over the previous centuries. Like the stock market on the eve of a Great Depression, we are living on inflated currency. God help us when the moral bubble bursts and an ethical recession sets in!

CHAPTER 15:

FROM TAO-LESS STUDENTS TO TAO-LESS CITIZENS

Although *The Abolition of Man* focuses primarily on the dangers of educating the young in a manner that both denies (and ridicules) the Tao and renders all aesthetic and ethical value judgments subjective, it does not confine itself solely to the classroom. Lewis is interested as well in the wider ramifications of the modernist attempt to mold its citizens apart from the Tao. As such, his book, though it begins with the educational and the aesthetic, slowly raises its sights to the social, the political, and the anthropological. Lewis's ultimate focus is not on children or young adults but on man as a species. What, in the end, will we make of ourselves and our world if we continue along a Tao-less trajectory? Earlier in this section, I discussed how Lewis (after Plato) constructs a metaphor in which each person is divided into head, belly, and chest. I would now like to shift to a second metaphor, one of my own making, which will help guide us as we steer our course away from the classroom toward the sociopolitical realm.

Picture, if you will, the figure of a man with his arms and legs spread outward in two large Vs (rather like the famous "Vitruvian man" of

Leonardo). Now imagine that man inscribed completely within a circle that presses down on him from all sides, even as he presses outward with his hands and feet. The forces that press down on him from the outside are the forces of fate, of duty, of honor, of responsibility: in short, all those "oughts" and "musts" that fix his identity and limit his actions and desires. The forces that flow outward from the man are the forces of free will, of choice, of self-assertion and personal autonomy: in short, all those individual passions and volitions that make each of us so radically unique. At times the external forces seem ready to crush the trapped figure inside; at times the internal forces seem ready to shatter the circle. But always the man holds up under the weight, and always the circle maintains its shape and integrity. The apostle Paul expresses it this way: "We are troubled on every side, yet not distressed; we are perplexed, but not in despair; persecuted, but not forsaken; cast down, but not destroyed" (2 Corinthians 4:8–9).

Each of us lives out our lives within that circle, now succumbing to its weight, now resisting it with all our willpower. The struggle is a hard one, and there are times when we are all tempted to step outside the circle. But this is the one thing we cannot do. For the circle is what defines us as human beings, what supplies us with our meaning and purpose, what keeps us centered, focused, and safe. Were we ever to find a way to step outside the circle, we would find that we had gained our freedom at the expense of our humanity. If we wanted to give that circle a name, we might call it, simply, the "Tao." Or, if we wanted to give it a more specifically biblical name, we might call it the "fear of the Lord."

In canto 3 of the *Inferno*, Dante and Virgil watch with horror and fascination as the souls of the damned gather round the boat of Charon, eager to be ferried across the river into hell. Dante asks who these souls are and how they came to this terrible place, and Virgil replies that all souls congregate here who in life lost the fear of God. The Old Testament tells us (many times) that the fear (or reverential awe) of the Lord is the beginning of wisdom. It is that which keeps us on track, which allows us to discern between the good and the bad, the virtuous and the vicious. When we lose that fear, we go off course, and our discernment grows dark and dull. Yes, we do, in one sense, become free, but it is a freedom that is finally self-destructive and dehumanizing. For the moment we cut ourselves loose from the oughts and the imperatives of God (and the Tao), we become enslaved to our own base, animal instincts.

Such is the fate of a man who steps outside the circle.

Such will be the fate of a society that attempts to do the same.

The last two-and-a-half centuries have witnessed numerous attempts by whole societies to step outside the circle: attempts to build a new, man-made utopia free from the oppressive weight of the Tao. In most cases, these would-be utopias ultimately metamorphosed into dystopias that bound rather than freed the dreams of their builders and reduced rather than expanded the human potential of those trapped within them. Indeed, I would argue, and I think that Lewis would agree, that all dystopic, totalitarian states (from Stalinist Russia to fascist Germany to Maoist China to Cambodia under the Khmer Rouge and France under Robespierre) are built and led by rulers who have put themselves outside the Tao and have seduced their people to do the same. This moving of an entire state or culture outside of the Tao is generally accomplished in one of two ways: either one part of the Tao is sacrificed in order to fulfill another part, or the Tao is rejected altogether and replaced by a new morality.

Whichever path is chosen on this dual road to dystopia, the end is always the same: death, despair, and dehumanization.

When God met Moses on Mount Sinai, he revealed to him, not one commandment and nine suggestions, but ten commandments, all of which were to be obeyed. Just so, the Tao is not made up of a selection of legal and ethical codes; it represents the full moral code as it has existed throughout time and across cultures. The Tao, that is to say, is a package, something that must be accepted in all its fullness and integrity; it is not a cafeteria, something from which we pick and choose only those bits that we like. Ethicists have long warned us that the ends do not justify the means, but they have not always couched their warning in terms of the

Tao. The *reason* why it is not ethical to rob from the rich in order to give to the poor is that the Tao-based command to care for the widow and the orphan does not override or negate the equally Tao-based prohibition against stealing. The Christian call to virtue (to following the Tao) does not (as Paul reminds us in Romans 3:8) authorize us to do evil that good may result. The activist who kills an abortion doctor in order to prevent the murder of an unborn child; the minister who marries a gay couple in the name of tolerance and mercy; the graduate who lies on his resumé in order to secure a job that will allow him to help others—all three have broken one part of the Tao in order to realize another part of it. Or, to be more precise, they have removed one element from the Tao and then treated that element as if it were the whole Tao.

In *The Four Loves*, C. S. Lewis warns us that whenever we take an earthly love (affection, eros, friendship) and make it into a god, it quickly becomes a demon. The phrases "God is love" and "love is God" may seem at first glance to be identical, but they are actually categorically opposed. To make the first statement is to assert (as does John in his first epistle) that one of the key qualities/activities of God is his love. As Lewis reminds us in *Mere Christianity* (book IV, chapter 4), when we say that God is love, we do not mean that he is the Platonic form of love (love with a capital "L"), but that he is love in action: for all eternity, the Father has loved the Son and the Son has loved the Father, and the Holy Spirit is himself that love embodied. As such, the statement "God is love" is both ethically and theologically rich; it captures a truth that cuts to the very core of the Christian faith. The statement "love is God," on the other hand, is both ethically impoverished and theologically deceptive. Those who make this oft-heard statement have not embraced the God who is love but have extracted one of the qualities *of* that God, and then treated that isolated quality as if it were itself God. Indeed, the finally disingenuous nature of their claim quickly becomes evident when they begin to justify their own unethical behavior in the name of this love deity they have created. Thus (like Paolo and Francesca in *Inferno* V), they commit adultery and then celebrate their sinful behavior as a pietistic act done, not for selfish, narcissistic reasons, but "for love." And why stop with adultery? Lying, cheating, stealing, and even murder can all be written off as so many sacrifices made at the altar of love.

The Bible has a word for this: *idolatry.*

Many in our modern age think that because they do not worship statues made of wood or stone, that they cannot be guilty of idolatry. They are wrong. Whenever we take anything from our human realm (even, and especially, something as good as love) and promote it to the level of God, we turn that thing into an idol, a false god in whose name anything can be justified. The same dynamic holds true when that good thing is a virtue extracted from the Tao. We have already seen above how modern public education has turned the three isolated virtues of tolerance, environmentalism, and egalitarianism into idols that must be obeyed, no matter what other virtues have to be suspended or broken. The popular *Godfather* films (in which the coveted virtue of family honor excuses theft, corruption, and murder) and genetic engineering (in which the golden calves of health and progress so often trump "lower" ethical concerns) offer two other seductive examples of how easy it is to fall prey to this particular brand of idolatry.

However, it is in the political realm that the dangers of this form of idolatry have been most fully realized. Most of the totalitarian regimes that rose up during the middle decades of the twentieth century justified their atrocities in the name of a virtue or ideal that they considered an absolute good. For the fascists, that virtue might best be defined as purity: the desire to ennoble an entire racial group by uniting their spirits, disciplining their bodies, and "cleansing" their genes. For the communists, it was the virtue of equality (or, better, egalitarianism) that served as the cornerstone of their sociopolitical revolution. Though the central virtue sought after by these politically antagonistic systems differs wildly, they are brutally alike in their willingness to break every other standard of ethics and morality in order to achieve that virtue. Thus, in Germany, the yearning for purity justifies the genocide of six million Jews, while in Russia, the yearning for equality justifies the massacre of untold numbers of middle-class farmers. The ends differ but the means are the same; Dachau and the Gulag are but two sides of the same coin. Still, though fascism and communism are both evils, I have always considered communism to be the greater, for the simple reason that it is more seductive and deceptive. Communism, that is to say, is the greater evil because, like Satan himself, it disguises itself as an angel of light. For most modern people, committed as they are to building an open, multicultural society, the ethnocentric vision of fascism carries little allure. But equality, that's a different story. Surely we must do all that we can to bring about a society in which fairness and equality are the rule. Yes, whatever it takes! Unfortunately, what it usually takes is the murder of a lot of people.

Again and again in his books and essays, Lewis warns us against the dangers of making an idol out of a single virtue. Indeed, the warning even finds its way into his fiction in the guise of villains who are as ruthlessly efficient in getting what they want as they are utterly convinced of the rightness (even selflessness) of their actions. In Lewis's very first novel, *Out of the Silent Planet* (published in 1938, on the brink of war), the antagonist, Weston, is not some crazed killer or greedy mercenary, but a learned scholar, a brilliant scientist, and a concerned humanitarian. He has come to Mars, not to enrich himself (as has his more typically villainous sidekick), but to further a high calling to which he has devoted his life and his talents: the preservation of the human race. To carry out this high calling, Weston is prepared to take any risk and to make any sacrifice necessary. As such, he possesses a kind of tragic nobility, not far removed from that of Jules Verne's Captain Nemo, who similarly vows himself to a high calling: the destruction of all mass weapons of war. Ironically, they are so monomaniacal in their commitment to life and peace that they end up destroying the very things they seek to preserve. Thus, just as Nemo is willing to blow up ships filled with innocent sailors in order to realize his goal, Weston is prepared to exterminate the inhabitants of Mars if it will ensure the survival of his species. Both are blind to the deep contradictions that underlie their ends and their means, their goals and their methods. They have each, in their own way, stepped outside the Tao and, by so doing, lost both their moral compass and their sense of outrage.

In *The Magician's Nephew*, written almost two decades later, Lewis offers his readers another would-be humanitarian. This time, however, his villain is far less noble or courageous: less a Promethean savior than a petty Faust who would risk (almost) anything for the sake of forbidden knowledge. I speak, of course, of Uncle Andrew, a vain, pedantic old bachelor who possesses a set of magic rings that he believes will take him into another world, but who is too cowardly to try the rings himself. Still, so devoted is he to uncovering the mysteries of those other worlds that he manipulates his young nephew (Digory) into going in his place. When Digory confronts his uncle with the evil of his actions, Andrew immediately silences the boy, lecturing him that great wisdom cannot be achieved without great sacrifice (by which, naturally, he means the sacrifice of Digory). "No, Digory," he explains, "Men like me who possess hidden wisdom are freed from common rules just as we are cut off from common pleasures. Ours, my boy, is a high and lonely destiny" (chapter 2). Digory, despite (or rather *because of*) his youth, sees right through this sham and thinks to himself: "All it means . . . is that he thinks he can do anything he likes to get anything he wants." Tragically, as in the story of the Emperor's New Clothes, adults (particularly *learned* adults) often miss that which is obvious to an innocent child. We promote and honor people like Uncle Andrew, calling them realists or strategic leaders or men who get things done. We are seduced by their vision, by their "high and lonely destiny," into making excuses for them, into allowing them to "bend the rules." And, needless to say, once we have convinced ourselves that we (or at least our party) share in that destiny, we are more than willing to make the same allowances for ourselves.

In his last novel, the strange and beautiful *Till We Have Faces*, Lewis takes up a third character who plays equally fast and loose with the Tao, but from a more densely psychological point of view. This time his "villain" is a lonely, ugly duckling Princess named Orual, who, though she becomes Queen, never becomes a swan. Ignored by her cruel father, Orual's central joy in life is raising and nurturing her younger half-sister, the beautiful Psyche. Orual feels deep affection for Psyche and lavishes all her love and attention on her. And yet, despite the depth of her affection, Orual makes decisions later in the novel that lead to the misery and destruction of Psyche. Like the overbearing mother in Lewis's *The Great Divorce*, who "loves" her son so much that she is willing to drag him out of heaven so that she can "care" for him properly in hell, Orual is blind to the fact that the idolatrous affection she feels for her sister is founded more on jealousy, pride, and control than on any type of agape (self-giving) love.

Though Orual moves in the circles of power and is a shrewd ruler, she might best be seen to represent a kind of feminine, domestic tyranny that is as destructive of lives as the more "masculine" tyranny represented by Weston and Andrew. Together, the Oruals and Westons make a misery of the world, forcing all others to bow along with them to the idol they have made. They are the divorced parents who sacrifice their children's innocence to their own needs for self-actualization; the politically correct professors who bend the minds of their students to fit the contours of their "liberal," multiculturalist agenda; the sadistic soldiers who torture prisoners for the sake of American "security."

They are those who make a desert and call it a peace.

CHAPTER 16:

THE SCIENTIST
AND THE MAGICIAN

I n the "case studies" discussed above, our antagonists all share the same willingness to break one part of the Tao in order to fulfill another part. But their method has not been the only one to do damage to the Tao. There have been (and will no doubt continue to be) others who are bolder in their schemes for social-political-moral reconfiguration. I speak of those whose goal it is to reject the Tao altogether and replace it with something new. Though this temptation to throw out the Tao and start again has, in a sense, always been with us, it received its greatest impetus (and authorization) during the eighteenth-century Age of Reason. Building on the work of earlier thinkers, such central Enlightenment philosophers as Hume, Kant, Voltaire, and Rousseau attempted to refound all things (from ethics to education to civil society) on secular, rational grounds. That is to say, they took the old humanism of the Middle Ages and Renaissance, which had sought the growth and perfection of man in a context that was either specifically Christian or at least closely allied to the goals and foundations of religion, and converted it into *secular* humanism. Moral codes revealed to prophets or implanted in man's conscience by God were to be replaced by a new "religion of reason" founded on logical, empirical principles. No longer was society to be shaped from on high by a preexisting code of morality; from now on, society would create her own civil religion, free from medieval "superstition" and that other antiquated notion, the "fear of the Lord." Man was all set to step outside the circle.

Indeed, no sooner had Hume et al. laid down their framework for a new type of philosophy and a new type of society than the "liberated" citizens of France (where the Enlightenment was strongest) attempted literally and politically to enact this new program. I speak, of course, of the French Revolution during its more advanced stages, when the Jacobins not only sent thousands of people to the guillotine but also enacted a massive program of social reengineering. In a symbolic break with their Judeo-Christian and Greco-Roman past, they changed the names of the months and then recalibrated the calendar to accord not with the birth of Christ but with the founding of the French Republic. The Revolution was to mark the dawn not only of a new civilization but of a new kind of man. At the height of revisionist fervor, a Cult of Reason was even instituted, replete with secularized versions of Catholic rituals and parades. Robespierre, fearing the still religious masses, modified this to include the worship of a Supreme Being, but this fully deistic god was but a pale imitation of the historically active, miracle-working, "accountability-expecting" God of the Old and New Testaments. From now on it was man, not God (secular reason, not the revealed Tao) that would be calling the shots.

Aghast at the excesses of the French Terror and perceiving the dangers inherent in its rejection of traditional morality, the British writer Edmund Burke, author of the liberal-Enlightenment *Philosophical Inquiry* discussed above, would forsake his early views to mature into one of the greatest defenders of conservatism and the Tao (best expressed in his *Reflections on the Revolution in France*). His country, however, though it would prove instrumental in defeating the Revolution's enfante terrible (Napoleon), would eventually assimilate (and domesticate) the same secular humanist spirit that made the Revolution possible. Thus, the more cautious nineteenth-century British Victorians (who inherited from France the role of Europe's cultural, military, and political trend-setter) would continue the Enlightenment/Jacobin dream of building a brave new world free from all the "superstitious errors" of the past, while keeping alive, as it were, the ghost of the Tao. Traditional morality would continue to thrive (at least on the surface), even as its foundations in the Tao were slowly whittled away. But no one seemed to notice. The great advances in communication, transportation, and industry that made London the capital not only of England but of a growing world empire proved a great distraction to those who might otherwise have seen what was happening. You see, like modern America, England had built up such a large reserve of moral capital that she was able to squander it for nearly a century without feeling the loss. The majority of the British public had, after all, been raised within the confines of the Tao, and, in any case, England's seemingly unending prosperity made it easy to wrap up God, country, and utopianism in a tidy little package.

Once the expansionist bubble burst, however, England found herself, in the closing decade of the century, morally and spiritually enervated. Once the carousel of progress had ground to a halt and her dreams of utopia had gone sour, England found herself both unwilling and unable to return to her roots in Christianity and the Tao. Though she experienced several revivals of traditional Christian faith and Tao-based morality throughout the century (from the low Protestantism of the Salvation Army to the high Anglicanism of the Oxford Movement), England as a nation found that she had drifted too far away from her old roots to return by the path whence she had come. Most of Europe joined England in her spiritual drift, as did most of the American elite (although the American people remained—and continue to remain—committed to revelation-based religion and morality). There was no going back; the only direction was forward. The question was not how do we rebuild Christendom, but how do we replace it with something more lasting and stable. Quo vadis: Where do we go from here?

Luckily for the West (and for the world in general), most of the twentieth-century attempts at sociopolitical engineering (from the educational reforms of the pragmatist John Dewey, to the New Deal of Franklin Roosevelt, to the European Union of today) followed in the more or less benign footsteps of the Victorians. That is to say, they moved forward in accordance with the methods and goals of secular humanism while paying what might be called "real lip service" to traditional morality. Or, to put it another way, they continued to act *as if* the ethical standards of the Tao were real and universal while theoretically denying that validity and refusing to allow it any status in their founding documents or their civil governance. Given another century, it is quite possible (alas, I think it quite probable) that this kinder, gentler road away from the Tao will lead to repression and atrocity, but at present its stores of moral capital are keeping it relatively on course.

But there is a darker path along which many of the "enlightened" heirs of secular humanism have traveled, a path that leads always and unstoppably to death, despair, and dehumanization. I discussed above how eighteenth-century epistemologists like Burke and Kant taught us that our responses to art are purely subjective and have nothing to do with the aesthetic object itself. I argued as well that once artistic taste becomes fully subjective—rather than being based on timeless standards—it is not long before all value judgments become equally subjective. Unfortunately, the Enlightenment's goal of converting first the arts and then traditional values from an objective to a subjective pursuit was accompanied by a second goal. At the same time that beauty and virtue were moved from the objective realm to the subjective, the natural world, which past ages had viewed subjectively, began to be treated as an object whose existence and meaning were wholly separate from our perceptions of it. The universe ceased to be a cathedral or a poem to be loved, contemplated, and admired and became instead a clockwork to be observed dispassionately.

For medieval Christians like St. Francis or Dante, the universe was our home, a place created by God to be in sympathy with us. For post-Enlightenment moderns, it is merely our house. Turning nature into an object has roots, of course, in the Renaissance, but then it also has roots in the materialistic theories and methods of the pre-Socratic philosophers of the sixth and fifth centuries BC. Even Newton, who admittedly was a key architect of the clockwork universe and who was probably more Unitarian/deist than Christian, still retained a faith in revelation and was able to perceive God's presence and design in the universe. After Newton, however, the whole wonderful classical-medieval-Renaissance model of the universe began to crumble. By 1800, nature had been cut loose from our perceptions of it, and by 1900, despite the futile attempts of the Romantics to reclaim nature as a companionable form, it had become a thing, a tool to be studied, manipulated, and controlled. Modern ethicists preach that we no longer have to adapt our behaviors and beliefs to fit the Tao, but that we can adapt the Tao to fit our behaviors and beliefs. Just so, modern scientists preach that we no longer have to adapt ourselves to the whims of nature; instead, we can use the miracle of technology to force nature to adapt itself to fit our whims.

It is one of the great ironies of our age that scientists often accuse Christians and other religious people of practicing magic, when, in fact, it is more often the scientists who dabble in the art of magic. To understand this irony, let us consider first the difference between prayer and voodoo. In the latter, the witch doctor believes that if he can just speak the right incantation or perform the proper spell, he can force nature (and often other people) to do his bidding. In the former, the Christian seeks not to force God's hand, but asks that God either grant his petition (if it is his will to do so) or give him the patience and faith to endure what he must. Magic, it need hardly be said, is far closer to voodoo than it is to prayer—as is science. "The serious magical endeavour," writes Lewis in chapter 3 of *The Abolition of Man*,

> and the serious scientific endeavour are twins: one was sickly and died, the other strong and throve. But they were twins. . . . For the wise men of old the cardinal problem had been how to conform the soul to reality, and the solution had been knowledge, self-discipline, and virtue. For magic and applied science alike the problem is how to subdue reality to the wishes of men: the solution is a technique; and both, in the practice of this technique, are ready to do things hitherto regarded as disgusting and impious—such as digging up and mutilating the dead.

Of course, we cannot exert such "magical" control over nature until we have objectified her and reduced her to an "it." Only then, when nature is no more to us than a toy train set, can we begin to rearrange and refit her to serve our desires and our lusts. "We reduce things to mere Nature," writes Lewis, "*in order that* we may 'conquer' them. . . . The price of conquest is to treat a thing as mere Nature."

I will admit that this desire to objectify and conquer nature has led to many advances in technology that have made our lives easier . . . but at what price? Aside from cutting us off from any real communion with nature, the Enlightenment goal of shaping nature on the lathe of science and reason has opened the door to something far more deadly. Just as the subjectivization of the arts eventually gave way to the subjectivization of values (and of religion in general), so the objectification of nature gave way, in turn, to the objectification of man. Once the universe had been reduced to a clockwork and nature to a machine, it was only a matter of time before man himself became reduced to one of the cogs in that machine. Lewis explains it thus:

> As long as this process [the objectification of nature] stops short of the final stage we may well hold that the gain outweighs the loss. But as soon as we take the final step of reducing our own species to the level of mere Nature, the whole process is stultified, for this time the being who stood to gain and the being who has been sacrificed are one and the same.

Once man becomes simply and solely a part of nature, then he can hardly be said to have gained any real mastery over nature. Indeed, when secular humanism is pushed to its logically illogical extreme, it becomes antihumanistic. Anyone familiar with the late nineteenth-century school of realism and naturalism (which includes novels by Zola in France, Thomas Hardy in England, and Frank Norris and Theodore Dreiser in America) will recognize how easily the radical secularism of a Marx or a Freud can rob us, in the end, of our humanity. In these dark, grim, finally godless novels, man is pressed down and becomes enslaved to the deterministic cycles of the animal (and even vegetable) world. Free will is crushed and man loses his innate, essential dignity: he is neither the special creation of a loving God nor the measure of all things nor even the crowning achievement of the evolutionary process. He is just a clothed beast fighting for survival, a poor forked animal stranded in a world without meaning or higher purpose. And as such, he is putty in the hands of any would-be dictator who would attempt to mold a new humanity apart from the blueprint of the Tao.

Francis Schaeffer, in his apologetics trilogy (*The God Who Is There, Escape from Reason, He Is There and He Is Not Silent*), has argued that modern man lives in a divided house with an upstairs and a downstairs that are radically separated from each other. In the (fully objective) downstairs, the realm of science and the "real" world, man is rational, but he is a machine, determined by forces he cannot control. In the (fully subjective) upstairs, the realm of religion and the arts, he is free but finally irrational. He cannot live in both stories at once. Either he lives his life in the (public, external) mechanistic downstairs and gives up his innate yearnings for any form of supernatural Truth or transcendent Beauty, or he leaps into the (private, internal) spiritual upper room and sacrifices all rational propositions and historical content. Decadence, relativism, and doctrine-less mysticism on the one hand; totalitarianism in all its forms on the other. Let us not forget that the totalitarian regimes of Hitler and Castro were directly preceded by a decade of unrestrained hedonism (that the decadence of the American Jazz Age was not followed by a similar regime is a testament not only to the foresight of our founding fathers but also to the fact that the great majority of Americans remained within the circle of the Tao and thus continued to be morally self-regulating). To live in the divided house of secular humanism leaves us with only two options: either we lose ourselves in a "higher" reality that is not real, or we surrender ourselves to become a cog in the machine. Either way, we cede much of that which makes us uniquely human. Body sacrificed to soul, or soul sacrificed to body.

You've come a long way, baby.

CHAPTER 17:

THE CHEST-LESS TYRANT

Where will it all end: this insidious process by which art and religion are reduced to mere feelings and nature and man to mere things? It will end, of course, in that same dystopic state that awaits those idolaters who convert one part of the Tao into the whole Tao. But, as dystopias go, it will be far worse. For, when the objectification of man combines with the utopian dreams of the eighteenth and nineteenth centuries and the scientific breakthroughs of the twentieth and twenty-first, then the foundation will be laid for a dystopia to end all dystopias. Then will the real experimentation and reengineering begin; then will the science of eugenics begin to reshape and remold man in accordance with the prevailing mood of the time. We will no longer ask if it is right or good or just or holy to remake man; we will ask only if it can be done and if doing so will increase efficiency and happiness. Apart from the Tao, what is to stop us? Indeed, since we will believe that what we are doing is for the good of mankind, we will be utterly remorseless in carrying it out. Once we step outside the Tao, there will be nothing left to tell us that this is the way man *should* be or *ought* to behave; all that will be left (to paraphrase both Machiavelli and Nietzsche) will be the crowd and those with the charisma (the will to power) to control it.

In one last radical assertion of free will, these charismatic leaders will oversee the remolding and reeducating of the next generation and, in the process, rob that generation (and the generations that follow) of its free will. They will be products, commodities, no more able to return to their original status than a mule can be transformed back into the horse or the ass from which it was bred. They may be physically stronger and less prone to disease; they may be better equipped to achieve the goals of their new utopian society. But if their leaders (Lewis calls them the Conditioners) no longer possess a fixed measure to tell them what is best and most proper for man, then who is to say that the goals for which they have been redesigned will be ones worth fulfilling.

For that matter, on what standard will the Conditioners base any of their decisions? They will be motivated neither by any set laws nor even by any sense of duty, for such words have no meaning apart from the Tao. For all their power over the masses, they will themselves be men without chests, men who cannot even delude themselves into believing (like Weston and Uncle Andrew) that they are fulfilling some higher calling or destiny. In the end, it will be their base desires (their belly) that will control them rather than their reason (their head). And when that happens, the human race, which thought to conquer nature by freeing itself from all moral restraint, will find itself her slave. Lewis's prophetic words (again from chapter 3) are worth quoting in full:

> It is from heredity, digestion, the weather, and the association of ideas, that the motives of the Conditioners will spring. Their extreme rationalism, by "seeing through" all "rational" motives, leaves them creatures of wholly irrational behaviour. If you will not obey the *Tao*, or else commit suicide, obedience to impulse (and therefore, in the long run, to mere "nature") is the only course left open.
>
> At the moment, then, of Man's victory over Nature, we find the whole human race subjected to some individual men, and those individuals subjected to that in themselves which is purely "natural"—to their irrational

impulses. Nature, untrammelled by values, rules the Conditioners and, through them, all humanity. Man's conquest of Nature turns out, in the moment of its consummation, to be Nature's conquest of Man. Every victory we seemed to win has led us, step by step, to this conclusion. All Nature's apparent reverses have been but tactical withdrawals. We thought we were beating her back when she was luring us on. What looked to us like hands held up in surrender was really the opening of arms to enfold us forever.

When we reduce ourselves to the level of nature, Lewis makes it clear, we end not in perfecting man but abolishing him! Our pursuit of "pure" reason and "pure" humanism detached from the Tao leads in the end to our being controlled by the irrational, dehumanizing forces of nature.

Of course, this prophetic truth was understood long ago by Plato. In the *Republic* (and elsewhere), Plato shows that the greatest tyrants are in fact the greatest slaves. Why and how this is so Socrates/Plato demonstrates with his own brand of remorseless logic. He begins (as is his custom) by asking a simple question: Who will tell the tyrant what to do; who, that is, will influence his decisions? Surely not the assembly, for the tyrant holds supreme power in the city and does not answer to the assembly (or to any other governing body). Surely not the law either, for the tyrant is above the law and can make or break it at will. Surely not even the gods, for the true tyrant puts himself above the gods as well. What then is left, if he obeys neither the people nor the laws nor the gods? There is only one thing left: the tyrant's own lusts and desires. But is it not our lusts and desires that lead us to make decisions that hurt and destroy us in the end? Yes, but in the absence of any law or standard to follow, the tyrant will have no recourse *but* to follow his lusts. He will, in fact, be a slave to his lusts, and, as such, he will be a slave to the worst possible taskmaster. The people, the laws, and the gods often direct us toward that which is beneficial not only to others but also to ourselves; but our lusts always, in the end, lead us to destruction. Yes, his lusts may direct the tyrant to perform a good act today if it catches his fancy, but they are just as likely to direct him tomorrow to do something evil.

Both Caligula and Nero began their reigns as popular monarchs loved by the people: mostly because their lusts and desires impelled them to shower the people with generosity. Unfortunately, their indiscriminate generosity soon left them weak and bankrupt and led them to replace their initial generosity with repressive policies. That this was so should not surprise us. Their former generosities were no more based on principles of charity or duty than were their latter atrocities. They simply responded as their external environment or internal desires prompted them at the moment. Just so, the Conditioner of Lewis's dystopia may grant his enemies mercy on one day and then execute twenty of his advisers on the next, not because of some ethical standard or rational program, but because yesterday the sun was shining brightly and there was a cool breeze and today he has a toothache. Again and again, our modern, secular humanist leaders tell us that our decisions must be based purely on reason (rather than the Tao), and yet, as we have seen, reason itself is the final casualty of our war against the Tao.

In chapter 2 of *The Abolition of Man*, Lewis calls this attempt to replace the revealed Tao with a new, man-made standard (based on reason, science, utilitarianism, egalitarianism, or what you will) the rebellion of the branches. "This thing," he writes,

> which I have called for convenience the Tao, and
> which others call Natural Law or Traditional Morality
> or the First Principles of Practical Reason or the First
> Platitudes, is not one among a series of possible systems
> of value. It is the sole source of all value judgements. If
> it is rejected, all value is rejected. If any value is retained,
> it is retained. . . . If the pursuit of scientific knowledge
> is a real value, then so is conjugal fidelity. The rebellion
> of the new ideologies against the Tao is a rebellion of
> the branches against the tree: if the rebels could succeed
> they would find that they had destroyed themselves.
> The human mind has no more power of inventing a
> new value than of imagining a new primary colour, or,

indeed, of creating a new sun and a new sky for it to move in.

Though *The Abolition of Man* was written several decades before the rise of postmodernism, Lewis accurately prophesies here what would become its core teaching: namely, that traditional, Judeo-Christian, "bourgeois" morality is but "one among a series of possible systems of value." Indeed, if it is modernism that most tempted us to remove one part of the Tao and convert it into the whole Tao, then it is postmodernism that now tempts us to throw out the Tao altogether and replace it with a new ideology of our own making. It is this postmodern spirit that lies behind the (finally irrational) belief on the part of many American and European leaders that if we can just purge the public square of all faith-based, revelation-based standards that a truly free and open society will result.

Or, to return to the central focus of this section, it is the spirit that believes (irrationally, suicidally) that if our institutions of learning could only be liberated from every trace of those same standards, the resulting generation of students would be empowered to rise up and build a brave new world. Of course, if our society ever did achieve this "promise" of a truly values-free education, it would find, like Lewis's rebellious branches, that it had cut itself off from the very tree that gives it life. If the Tao dies, then so do all those values and virtues that supply humanity with the motives and the will to build a free and open society: the intrinsic, essential worth of every human life, charity, self-sacrifice, duty, hope, and so on. Educated apart from these values (and, Lewis reminds us—contra Nietzsche—we lack the power to invent new ones), that brave new generation will either abdicate its social responsibilities in favor of pure self-interest, or (with the help of values-free genetics) build the state described above: a dystopia led by Conditioners who make their decisions, not on the basis of some universal Geneva Convention (itself meaningless apart from the Tao), but on heredity, digestion, and the weather.

CHAPTER 18:

THE DEATH OF LANGUAGE

B efore closing this section, let us consider one final danger of a values-free education that has equally wide-ranging, sociopolitical ramifications and that reflects the postmodern (rather than the modern) attack on the Tao—the decay of language. Since the days of Socrates and the sophists, philosophers have debated the status of language, questioning whether words like *justice* or *truth* or *beauty* point back to a real, transcendent meaning or are merely arbitrary sounds reflecting a limited man-made (or "polis-made") meaning. Until the twentieth century, the great majority of people gravitated toward the former view, trusting that behind a word like *truth* was something fixed and universal (the Platonic Form of Truth). The fact that this absolute, "supralexical" standard existed did not guarantee that anytime we used the word truth that we were capturing (or even approximating) that standard, but it did guarantee a final resting point for meaning and a final limit to infinite regress. Words do not mean whatever we want them to mean (as Humpty Dumpty insists); they have a meaning that exists apart from us and our cultural and grammatical systems. For the Christian, the reason that the Bible (the Word of God) carries the same authority in whatever language into which it is translated is that its meaning ultimately rests not on a single linguistic structure but on the eternal Word of God (Christ). The written Word is a conduit for and a mirror of the divine Word (that the divine Word is also living, active, and personal is something Plato did not know, for it had not yet been revealed).

In most of the universities (and even many of the seminaries) of our day, the preceding five sentences would be considered not only erroneous but also hopelessly naive. Just as our age has lost its faith in the transcendent, cross-cultural status of the Tao, so has it lost its faith in the ability of language to embody truth. The two losses are, of course, directly related. If the dictates of our conscience are arbitrary, then so are the words that fall from our lips. If we can no longer accept the call of virtue as binding (as something we *ought* to do), then how can we ascribe any final, ultimate meaning to words like *courage* or *chastity* or *love*? The relationship between the debunking of the Tao and the decay of language is not only a chronological one; it is causal as well. One leads naturally to the other: not just philosophically, but practically.

Once a nation or a party or an organization cuts itself loose from the Tao, it is only a matter of time before it starts manipulating words to cloak its real motives and designs. Lewis embodies this tragic truth subtly but effectively in the third installment of his Space Trilogy, *That Hideous Strength*. Just as this novel exposes what happens when the Good, the True, and the Beautiful are abandoned (see chapter 3, above), so does it expose the dangers of abandoning the Tao. Indeed, *That Hideous Strength* may be profitably read and interpreted as a fictionalized embodiment of the prophetic warnings laid out in *The Abolition of Man* (the former was published two years after the latter). In the novel, Lewis presents us with the National Institute of Co-ordinated Experiments (or N.I.C.E.), a secret society with plans to build the very dystopia Lewis describes in *The Abolition of Man*. Into its ranks, the N.I.C.E. recruits Mark Studdock, a sociologist whose desperate desire to be on the "inside" and whose skepticism toward religion and the Tao make him a very useful pawn. In the absence of any fixed ethical standard against which to measure the goals and practices of the N.I.C.E., Mark accepts, naively and uncritically, its full program of "liberal" reform, scientific experimentation, and social reengineering. Indeed, so willingly and willfully is he deceived that he agrees to compose propaganda articles for the N.I.C.E. to put a clean public face on its atrocities (chapter 6.4). Mark is a professor and a humanist, and his wife is a graduate student of literature (she is writing a dissertation on John Donne); yet, despite the centrality of the word to their educations and careers, he feels no guilt or remorse manipulating and perverting words in order to cover up for an organization whose acronym is itself a grotesque euphemism.

In the end, the N.I.C.E is defeated with the help of the guardian spirits of the planets, including the spirit of Mercury. Mercury (whose Greek name, Hermes, lies at the root of the word *hermeneutics*: the science of interpreting the true meaning of Scripture) brings with him not power or love, but Language, the pure, prefallen language of Adam. In this language, Lewis tells us, "meanings were not given to the syllables by chance, or skill, or long tradition, but truly inherent in them as the shape of the great Sun is inherent in the little waterdrop" (10.4). During the final, climactic battle, Mercury descends on the headquarters of the N.I.C.E. Confronted by what Lewis calls (perhaps with Donne in mind) "the white-hot furnace of essential speech" (15.1), the leaders of the N.I.C.E are thrown into disarray and begin to speak gibberish (the title of the novel is taken from a poem about the Tower of Babel). Having destroyed all moral and linguistic standards, the N.I.C.E. is reduced in the end to irrationality, its deconstructed speech giving way to a bloodbath as the leaders execute each other in an orgy of violence. The death of the Tao and the death of the Word turn out to be essentially the same act: both resulting in the murder of humanism and humanity.

That Hideous Strength, published in the final year of WWII, offers us a warning not dissimilar from another dystopic novel, written by an exact contemporary of Lewis, George Orwell. In *1984*, Orwell shows, even more effectively than Lewis, what happens to language and meaning in a society that has replaced the Tao with a new morality of its own making. Indeed, though Orwell was essentially an atheist (if a genial one), he saw as clearly as Lewis that the rejection of all set standards of decency on the part of fascists, communists, and imperialists had helped to foster a growing plague of political euphemism. Orwell argues in "Politics and the English Language" that in the twentieth century politics had become "largely the defense of the indefensible." Because of this (because politics so often tried to work outside the boundaries of the Tao), the language of politics had come

> to consist largely of euphemism, question-begging and sheer cloudy vagueness. Defenseless villages are bombarded from the air, the inhabitants driven out into the countryside, the cattle machine-gunned, the huts set on fire with incendiary bullets: this is called *pacification*. Millions of peasants are robbed of their farms and sent trudging along the roads with no more than they can carry: this is called *transfer of population* or *rectification of frontiers*. People are imprisoned for years without trial, or shot in the back of the neck or sent to die of scurvy in Arctic lumber camps: this is called *elimination of unreliable elements*.

To these examples, we could add many others: the totalitarian regimes of East Germany and China called themselves the German Democratic Republic and the People's Republic of China, respectively; Hitler called his genocide of the Jewish race the "Final Solution," and his heirs refer to the process as ethnic cleansing; those who advocate the murder of unborn children call their position pro-choice, while those who would exclude Judeo-Christian beliefs and ethics from the classroom do it in the name of diversity. It is wrong to torture prisoners, but if we extract vital information from enemy insurgents, then we can circumvent (and thus ignore) both the Tao and language itself.

Two years after writing "Politics and the English Language," Orwell went on to create an entire language of political euphemisms known as Newspeak, a masterpiece of serious, prophetic satire that Lewis considered the best part of *1984* (see his essay "George Orwell," anthologized in *On Stories*). Fashioned by the totalitarian Conditioners of Oceania as a means of controlling both the bodies and the minds, actions and thoughts of the conditioned, Newspeak goes far beyond the simple examples of political euphemism listed above. The true goal of the language, explains Orwell in "The Principles of Newspeak" (which he appended to *1984*), is not just to cover up atrocities committed by the ruling party, but "to *diminish the range of thought.*" Orwell (like Lewis) knew that as corporeal beings who inhabit space and time, we are strongly influenced by the words we use and the images those words convey. If the word *freedom* (and all its synonyms and cognates) did not exist, it would be difficult (if not impossible) for us to conceive of the concept of freedom. (That is not to say that freedom is "merely" a word, only that our physical brains need the word to embody the meaning; just so, the real but invisible God made himself known to us through his incarnate Logos/Word/Son.) By "eliminating" from Newspeak all "undesirable words and by stripping such words as remained of unorthodox meanings, and so far as possible of all secondary meanings whatsoever," the rulers of Oceania ensure that any and all resistance will be crushed at the linguistic level of thought itself. Or, to express it in the terms of this section, the next logical step after man and nature have been reduced to things is to objectify language as yet another cog in the modernist-secularist, antihumanistic machine.

Though the Western world has (thankfully) not yet fallen into the reductionism of Newspeak, signs of its coming abound. During the last two decades of the twentieth century, many liberal secular universities in America instituted speech codes to forbid the use of language considered by the establishment Conditioners to be racist or sexist. Canada has threatened to prosecute pastors who preach that homosexuality is a sin; the charge: hate crime. Nearly all students who come out of academia these days have been brainwashed into using the word "text" to refer to all written forms of expression (and often nonwritten ones as well). The reason behind this academic brainwashing (carefully obscured by those promoting the postmodern agenda) is to nudge students away from the traditional ranking of genres into a radically egalitarian view that treats all forms of expression as possessing equal value. No text is to be privileged over (or granted more inherent, lasting worth than) any other text. A novel by Dickens, an issue of the *New York Times*, a piece of pornography from the Internet, the lyrics of a rap song, the *Iliad* of Homer, a TV sitcom—all are to be accorded the same worth (which means, in the end, that all are equally worthless). None of the works listed in the preceding sentence lies closer to "Truth" or "Beauty"; none is to be criticized for violating standards of decency or morality. They are all just . . . well . . . texts.

However, the most ubiquitous (and pernicious) alteration of our language, one that has spread almost universally through our public schools and colleges, is to be seen in the way that students of all ages are encouraged (if not outright forced) to alter their speech and writing patterns to reflect the "principles" of gender-neutral language (many academic journals will not print essays that refuse to conform to these principles). Indeed, so successful have been the promoters of this feminist agenda that they have even convinced otherwise traditional (and sensible) Christians to bend and butcher their books, their sermons, their liturgies, their hymnals, and their Bible translations to fit the Procrustean bed of what they (euphemistically) call "gender-accurate language." The mandates of this feminist version of Newspeak are well known: never use "he" as the gender-inclusive pronoun; replace "sexist" words like *fireman* and *policemen* with gender-neutral ones like *firefighter* and *police officer*; use *brothers and sisters* rather than *brothers* or *brethren*; use the plural whenever possible so as to avoid having to use *he/she* (since using "he" is already forbidden by mandate number one). Taken together, these mandates have helped increase the growing awkwardness, vagueness, and downright ugliness of most academic and corporate writing, while championing a particularly petty form of egalitarianism (on par with envious siblings who each insist on getting *exactly* the same size piece of pie). They have also helped collapse gender distinctions that are essential not only to the proper functioning of society, marriage, and child rearing, but also to the nurturing and fostering of that wonderful and mysterious masculinity and femininity implanted in us by that God who (unlike the postmodern literati) *really* appreciates diversity.

And that's not all! There is one final casualty of gender-neutral language that, as far as I can tell, has yet to be fully considered. Since language began, people have referred to the human race by the words "man" or "mankind." But no more, at least if the feminists, and those who have been unconsciously conditioned by them, have their way. Now *man/mankind* is to be replaced by *humankind* or *humans* or *persons* or

THE DEATH OF LANGUAGE

some other locution. Aside from the aforementioned ugliness of this practice, the refusal to use *man/mankind* has had the subtle effect of not only neutering but also dehumanizing language. When a reader reads the word *man* (or *mankind*), an image of a real, concrete man pops into his head. When he reads *human* or *person*, something far more abstract (and certainly less noble) is conjured instead, something that more closely parallels the impersonal, amorphous god of pantheism than the personal, incarnate God of Christianity. Now, of course, this is the very *reason* that feminists want us to use the word *person* rather than *man*. They reject any and all notions of headship, including the Pauline practice of imaging and summing up all (fallen) humanity in the person of Adam. They would far prefer for us to imagine in our minds a neutered, face-less, androgynous thing than have our thoughts directed to the image of a male. Likewise, they would prefer us to use "it" rather than "she" when referring to single or collective objects toward which we feel love and affection: ships, countries, churches, etc. (Mother Rome is no more acceptable than Father God). The only exception allowed to this rule is the absolutely juvenile practice of alternating male and female names for hurricanes: not even the most petty, envious, prepubescent child could have thought that one up!

Now, let me add one caveat here. Just as the gay activists will claim that gay marriage merely represents a natural evolution in social and sexual relationships, so will the feminists claim that gender-neutral language merely marks a natural progression in the evolution of English. Both claims are false. There is nothing "natural" about either: both are artificial changes imposed by a minority in accordance with a personal/political agenda. Both "innovations" are less like the loss (except in Texas!) of the second-person plural pronoun ("y'all") and more like the attempt by the French revolutionaries to change the calendar to reflect their radical, anti-Tao ideology.

If you think I'm exaggerating all this, just pick up a modern hym-nal or Bible translation; or, better yet, read through your children's (or grandchildren's) textbooks. You will find that the word *man* (in the sense of mankind) has been banished altogether (even the term *man-made* has been excised). You will find, more generally, a flattening of language, a dulling of wonder, a stifling of joy. You will find the slow pressing down of true diversity into a colorless, genderless, classless egalitarianism: a lowest-common-denominator world devoid of Beauty and Truth. Indeed, if you look really close, you will see the seeds of the abolition of man.

Though, beware, you may not recognize them at first. Best instead to look for phrases such as the following: "the sociopolitical evolution of humankind through genetic engineering," "sensitivity training," and "lifestyle experimentation."

Dare I say it again? You've come a long way, baby.

PART IV

ASLAN IN THE ACADEMY

CHAPTER 19:

RESTORING THE PAST

A cademia is a great place for dropping names. Indeed, many times a day, whether it be in a classroom, the faculty lounge, or the library, I will overhear the names of one or more of the great thinkers of the past. And when I hear those names, my mind generally makes a quick and singular association. I hear Plato, and I think Greek philosopher; I hear Tolstoy, and I think Russian novelist; I hear Wordsworth, and I think British Romantic poet. Sometimes, a name will conjure a double association (I hear Hemingway, and I think both American novelist and war correspondent), but, generally, the first image (novelist in the case of Hemingway) will quickly prevail over the second. This mental phenomenon, however, does not occur when I hear the name of C. S. Lewis. With the invocation of that name, three separate and distinct images immediately rise up in my mind, each jockeying for position over the other: Christian apologist; sci-fi/ fantasy writer; Oxbridge don. Who *was* this man who humbly referred to himself as Jack? Was he the popular writer of *Mere Christianity* and *The Screwtape Letters*, the ingenious creator of The Chronicles of Narnia and The Space Trilogy, or the scholarly author of *The Allegory of Love*

149

and *A Preface to Paradise Lost*? Was he an evangelist, a novelist, or a lecturer? Saint, fantasist, or critic?

Of course, he is all three, but this common-sense observation does not release us from the obligation to at least try to reconcile the three aspects of his unique vocation. Although such a reconciliation could be effected in a number of different ways, I would like to offer in what follows one particular (and personal) way that rests upon those aspects of my own vocation that I share with Lewis. For, like Jack, I am a Christian English professor who divides his time equally between speaking and writing on apologetics and literature and who has written his own trilogy of children's novels. It is through such vocational eyes that I see the world, and, when I cast those same eyes on the life and works of C. S. Lewis, I see a single, composite picture form: that of a dedicated teacher who, with the same synthetic, shaping imagination he brought to Narnia, creatively integrated his public, academic role as professor and scholar with his private, personal identity as follower of Christ and defender of the faith.

In short, I see a professional who bravely and consistently refused to abide by the modernist (post-Enlightenment) notion of a professional as one who separates completely the public from the private sphere. That is not to say that Lewis shared the personal details of his life with his students or that he delivered sermons in the classroom (he did neither), but that he questioned the way the modern world *defined* the spheres of public and private. Increasingly since the eighteenth century, the Western world has driven a (finally artificial) wedge between reason and revelation—between scientific facts, logical proofs, and secular institutions on the one hand and religious beliefs, spiritual values, and faith-based communities on the other. The former, we have all been taught to believe, must dominate the public arena (the "naked public square" to use Richard John Neuhaus's apt phrase), while the latter must remain safely walled up in the private, domestic sphere. The two must never be allowed to overlap. Indeed, anyone who brings his "private" religious beliefs into the "public" square (politics, education, media, etc.) risks being dismissed as nonprofessional, nonrational, nonobjective, and, perhaps, nonsensical. The claims of faith are all well and good behind church doors and in the sanctity of one's prayer closet—just make sure they do not (like radiation from a nuclear power plant) leak out into the public streets of the city. Recite your creed on Sunday morning, but don't let it follow you into the workweek.

For Lewis, such an unnatural and arbitrary separation of the sacred from the secular, the Christian from the humanist, simply would not do. He would insist (in his apologetics, in his fantasy novels, and in his scholarly work) that the integrated Christian worldview that reigned in Europe for a millennia and a half was not only rationally and logically sound but also deserved a voice in the public (and especially academic) arena. It is *this* Lewis whom I spy at the core of his multifaceted vocation, a Lewis from whom we desperately need to hear today.

Granted, much work has been done over the last several decades to encourage Christians not to compartmentalize their faith, but to carry it with them into the workplace: to be, that is, salt and light in the (secular) world. Some of this work has even targeted the educational sphere. Nevertheless, despite the growth of such groups as the Conference of Christian Colleges and Universities and the C. S. Lewis Foundation, many Christian educators still feel at a loss when they are challenged (from without or within) to combine their faith and teaching in an effective, winsome way. It is for just such beleaguered Christian educators—whether they be grammar or high school teachers, college professors or ministers of education, youth pastors or homeschool moms—that I offer the following overview of what C. S. Lewis can teach the modern Christian engaged in the vital work of nurturing, shaping, and challenging the minds of the young.

First and foremost, if the Christian educator is to follow in the footsteps of C. S. Lewis, then he must learn to identify and resist what Lewis (after Owen Barfield) called "chronological snobbery." As should be clear to anyone who has eyes to see, we live in an age that is grossly self-satisfied with its own achievements and beliefs. True, every age likes to see itself as the culmination of all the ages that came before it, but what distinguishes our age (and the wider modernist age in general) is its tendency to dismiss all past ages as unenlightened, misguided, and "medieval." The problem is not our cocky claim that we know more facts and figures about the natural world than our forefathers or that we possess more gadgets than our preindustrialized predecessors. The fact of the matter is we do. No, the problem is that *because* we know and have more "stuff," we (illogically) reason that our own philosophical, theological, and aesthetic views; our own prioritizing of divine, human, and civic virtues; and our own social, economic, and educational initiatives must necessarily be superior to theirs.

In chapter 13 of his spiritual autobiography, *Surprised by Joy*, Lewis defines chronological snobbery as "the uncritical acceptance of the intellectual climate common to our own age and the assumption that whatever has gone out of date is on that account discredited." He then follows up this definition by challenging himself and his readers to question their "uncritical acceptance" of their own age by doing the following:

> You must find why it went out of date. Was it ever refuted (and if so by whom, where, and how conclusively) or did it merely die away as fashions do? If the latter, this tells us nothing about its truth or falsehood. From seeing this, one passes to the realization that our own age is also "a period," and certainly has, like all periods, its own characteristic illusions.

It is a sad fact that we who are Christians and educators are often the *last* people to question the philosophical, theological, and aesthetic history presented in our textbooks. We accept (as unreflectively as our non-Christian counterparts) the "party line" that claims our age no longer believes what our ancestors believed because those old beliefs were put to the test and found to be flawed and in error. It's not hard to see why we accept this line. After spending four years in undergraduate school (and often many more in various graduate programs) absorbing the modernist reading of history, we are often reluctant to take the time and effort to question the assumptions and presuppositions on which that reading rests. Our job we feel is simply to pass on to our charges that which was taught to us as a proven, objective thing; to do otherwise would cause uncomfortable cognitive dissonance and leave us open to the charge of unprofessionalism, nonprogressivism, and (worst of all) naiveté. Yes, we will question some of the details, but we too often and too quickly accept as a given the overarching framework of the received reading.

Again, every generation of educators has certainly been guilty to some degree of accepting without question the official history, but our age has put a new twist on such uncritical acceptance of the reigning paradigm. Lewis explains it best in chapter 12 of *Reflections on the Psalms*: "Between different ages there is no impartial judge on earth, for no one stands outside the historical process; and of course no one is so completely enslaved to it as those who take our own age to be, not one more period, but a final and permanent platform from which we can see all other ages objectively." If there is one thing our age is guilty of, it is precisely this stubbornly held belief that we have a clear vision of all the flaws of every age, including our own. Even Marxist-inspired critics (feminists, new historicists, etc.), who pride themselves on their ability to pierce through all bourgeois illusions to discern the "real" socioeconomic forces that determine thought and action, willfully ignore the fact that if their method is correct, then they themselves (and their method) are likewise products of socioeconomic forces over which they have no conscious control.

Much of the problem can be traced to a logical fallacy that lies at the very heart of our modernist self-delusion: namely, the argument that scientific progress parallels moral progress. The analogy asserted between these two types of progress is, of course, a false one, but it exerts a great deal of emotional and rhetorical force. "Look at the great medical and technological breakthroughs that have occurred during our age," the spiel goes. "We have found cures for countless diseases, greatly reduced the infant mortality rate, vastly increased the speed of transportation and communication, and multiplied a hundredfold the most basic creature comforts. Surely an age that has accomplished such things must also be morally advanced; surely the refinement in bodily pleasures achieved in our age suggests a concurrent refinement of aesthetics and spirituality." In order to give the lie to this line of thought, we need simply remember that the foundations for all these advances were laid out in the decades *before* "morally advanced" totalitarian rulers from the right and the left began their wholesale slaughter of a significant percentage of the human race.

Professor Lewis devoted considerable time and energy to exploding the rampant chronological snobbery lurking behind such false analogies. In his scholarly work, his apologetics, and even his fiction, he argued passionately that newer does not always means better; that though progress may be the rule for evolution, technology, and consumerism, neither culture nor religion nor ethics can be so measured. For Lewis this argument invariably involved a defense of the Middle Ages, since the modern world more often than not defines its achievements (and its superiority) over against those of the so-called Dark Ages. By defending medieval Christendom from its detractors (both inside and outside the church), Lewis would be defending as well the specifically Christian worldview on which that age rested and upon which modern Europe was built.

In mounting his defense of the Middle Ages, Lewis set himself two related tasks. First, in *The Discarded Image* (and elsewhere), he systematically exposed Enlightenment propaganda tactics that have profoundly, and falsely, shaped our view of the medievals. Chief among these tactics was the "fact," disseminated by Voltaire in Europe and Washington Irving in America, that all the medievals firmly believed that the earth was flat. Lewis swiftly demolishes this false "fact"—one that is consistently taught in our schools, both public and private—by quoting passages from a host of ancient and medieval writers (Aristotle, Ptolemy, Boethius, Aquinas, Dante) who knew full well that the world was round. In a similar vein, Lewis also quotes the medievals themselves on another subject obscured by Enlightenment propaganda: the relative size and value of the earth. Though modern teachers, in unwitting collusion with the eighteenth-century *philosophes*, continue to inform their students that the men of the "Dark Ages" thought the universe was a small, cozy place dominated by the all-important earth, the fact is they knew the universe was vast (though not infinite) and that in relation to that vastness the earth was but an insignificant point. Furthermore, the medieval belief (based on empirical observation) that the earth was at the center of the universe was not put forth as proof of human superiority (they left *that* claim to the more arrogant, egocentric thinkers of our modern world), but as a sobering reminder that we are the darkest, heaviest, coldest point in the cosmos, the drainage ditch of the universe. (If you don't believe me—or Lewis—on this point, just read your Dante!)

Lewis was not appointed honorary head of the Oxford Socratic Club for nothing. Like Plato's great teacher, Lewis knew how to crush baseless arguments and wrestle logical fallacies to the ground. He did not, however, confine himself to such negative criticism. There was a positive side as well to Lewis's two-pronged defense of the Middle Ages. Not content merely to point out the flaws in our modern perception of that misunderstood age, Lewis sought (again, in his academic work, his apologetics, and his fiction alike) to rehabilitate the medieval cosmological model as a thing of beauty worthy of contemplation. He offered, that is, a countervision, an alternate narrative to the one taught in our colleges and schools. Just as Charles Dickens used his beloved *A Christmas Carol* to breathe new life and joy into the dull Yuletide celebrations of the overly utilitarian Victorians, so did Lewis use his equally beloved Chronicles of Narnia to help revive in us jaded, overly materialistic moderns a sense of wonder, humility, and, yes, thankfulness before the awesome majesty of God's creation.

May we not, as modern Christian educators, join Lewis in his mission to restore to our world a lost sense of its own sacred past? I would argue that we must. How long can we go on trying to convince our students that the teachings of Christ and the church are both true and universally valid, while passively perpetuating the Enlightenment myth that the long age during which Christendom reigned in Europe was dark, brutal, and superstitious. To be more specific, if we are Catholic believers, then we must stop being embarrassed by all the bad press and seek to recapture the rich cultural, intellectual, and aesthetic heritage of the Latin Church. If we are Protestant Christians, then we need to "fess up," once and for all, to the sad fact that the secular *philosophes* would never have been able to spread their propaganda over Europe had they not been assisted by anti-Catholic reformers eager to slander their spiritual competitors. (Contrary to popular opinion, Protestant propaganda has historically been nastier and more effective than Catholic propaganda.) It's time that we set the record straight, time that we reclaimed what was good and noble and virtuous in the Middle Ages.

We might start by encouraging our students to approach the Middle Ages from the inside, rather than the outside. That is to say, let them read Dante's *Divine Comedy* and Chaucer's *Canterbury Tales*, not just as literary relics of a bygone era, but as windows on a world both wondrously strange and strangely familiar. Let them see (*really* see) that the Christians who lived back then were real people who fought real struggles and that it was out of their struggles that Europe was born.

And while we're at it, we just might try to reclaim as well America's brief experiment with Christendom: the Puritan Age. For over a century now, we have been indoctrinated by Nathaniel Hawthorne, Perry Miller, and Max Weber into viewing the Puritans as neurotic, hypocritical prudes driven to succeed by their own spiritual and psychological insecurities. When will our Christian academies produce historians with enough courage to at least question this monolithic view? These God-inspired and Christ-haunted Puritans were as much founding fathers of our democratic institutions and our national soul as were Washington, Jefferson, Adams, or Franklin. Yet they continue to remain outsiders, sullied, in great part, by a single event (the Salem Witch Trials) that has been blown out of all proportion. Yes, some very good work has been done on Jonathan Edwards, but American Christians have yet to challenge in any real way (in a way, that is, that affects how our children are taught and how our nation views itself) the official, *Scarlet Letter* view of the Puritan Age.

CHAPTER 20:

THE RENAISSANCE
NEVER HAPPENED

O nce we, as Christian educators, have given ourselves permission to look upon the past with sympathetic eyes, we are ready to follow Lewis one step further in his vocation of rehabilitation. Lewis knew that if he was to secure for Europe's Christian heritage a legitimate voice in the modernist arena, he would have to question not only the status of the medieval age itself, but also its relative position and function in the stages of European history. This Lewis did brilliantly in the inaugural lecture he delivered at Cambridge University in 1954 to initiate his tenure there as the chair of medieval and Renaissance literature. In the address (anthologized under the title "De Descriptione Temporum"), Lewis critiques the firmly held (indeed, unquestioned) belief that with the birth of the Renaissance, Europe left behind her ignorance and obscurantism and moved forward into the modern world. In opposition to this view (and the prejudices that underlie it), Lewis boldly proclaimed that the Renaissance, far from parting company with the Middle Ages, never really happened. What we call modernism did not begin in 1500 but in the eighteenth century; it was the secular ideals of the Enlightenment, not the rebirth of classical culture, that defined Europe's break with her Christian (and classical) past. In fact, if truth be told, the Renaissance stands closer to the medieval and classical world in its view of man, God, and the universe, than any of these ages do to our modern, post-Enlightenment world. Or, to put it another way, Michelangelo, Cervantes, Shakespeare, and Milton have more in common with Dante, Virgil, and Plato than with Voltaire or John Stuart Mill or Darwin. Even freethinkers like Galileo, Bacon, and Montaigne would surely have found greater kinship with the medievals than with the moderns.

We do not necessarily have to agree fully with Lewis in his contention that the Renaissance never happened to second him in his attempt to reenvision the historical dynamics that shaped the Western world. But if we wish to be true to his legacy, then we must be willing to give each age its due, to see it as it was in itself, rather than to view it through the distorting lens of a later age that was hostile to it. If we are feeling in a bold mood, we might start by reassessing the Spanish Inquisition. As more of the records documenting that period have come out, it has become increasingly clear that the Inquisition (at least the part overseen by the church) was no where near as bloody as long-standing Protestant and secular Enlightenment propaganda (not to mention Monty Python) has led us to believe. The death count was, in fact, quite low (especially when compared to the atrocities perpetrated in England and France in the name of religion). But the myth persists, perhaps in part because the period that includes the Inquisition marks a decisive moment when Spain was asserting her Catholic identity over against Moorish oppression from the South. As Spanish philosopher Julian Marías has pointed out, Spain is one of the few countries in Europe that made a direct and self-conscious decision to be a Christian nation defined in part by her Christian creeds.

And speaking of Christian self-identity, where shall we find Christian historians and educators brave enough to revive, as a positive thing, the image of the Christian knight risking his life in defense of Christendom and the Holy Land? No, we should not cover over the atrocities perpetrated during the Crusades, but it is high time we remembered who exactly the aggressors were. The knights were there to liberate lands that had been seized by Muslim conquerors. (Ironically, in the Middle East today, it is the Palestinians and not the Israelis who are following in the footsteps of the crusaders!) Simply consider that the armies of Islam had seized control of all seven cities mentioned in Revelation 2–3 (that is, the original, most ancient centers of Christianity), and you will begin to see what an outrage the Muslim occupation of the Holy Land meant to the medieval Christians. Lewis reminds us in part I, chapter 2 of *Mere Christianity* that the reason we no longer kill witches is not because we are more moral than our ancestors, but because we no longer believe in witches. If we did believe in them, writes Lewis, "if we really thought that there were people going about who had sold themselves to the devil and received supernatural powers from him in return and were using these powers to kill their neighbours or drive them mad or bring bad weather, surely we would all agree that if anyone deserved the death penalty, then these filthy quislings did." In the same way, let us not consider ourselves less violent than the crusaders because we no longer believe it a valid thing to fight for the honor of sacred ground.

I mention the Spanish Inquisition and the Crusades in particular, since these two events have, for the last two hundred years, functioned in secular academic circles as handy justifications for dismissing out of hand the true legacy of Christendom. Indeed, these two events (along with ritual invocations of the bad popes) have been used to blacken Christianity's reputation vis-à-vis the sociopolitical realm in the same exact way that the trial of Galileo and the Scopes Monkey Trial have been used to blacken Christianity's reputation vis-à-vis science. In this arena, the church has, thankfully, raised up a handful of crusading scholars and teachers to remind us that the so-called war between science and religion is a modern and finally artificial thing. If not orthodox Christians, all the great early modern scientists (from Galileo to Newton to Kepler) were at least theists who shared a theistic worldview. Indeed, they would not have devoted their lives and careers to discovering or, better, uncovering the laws of nature, if they had not believed that the universe was a rational, ordered system created by a rational, ordered God. There is no such thing as an indigenous Hindu or Buddhist science, not because the holders of those religions lacked critical-thinking skills or technological know-how, but because they did not share the Christian faith *in* a rational universe.

Too often, Christian educators grow timid and weak-kneed when the Crusades or the trial of Galileo is mentioned. Rather than confront these events head-on and seek to place them in a wider context, we either accept (passively) the standard view or reject (defensively) the whole issue and withdraw into our Christian subculture. And the reason we do this is because we can't take on the individual events themselves without first wrestling with the received interpretation of how these events fit into the stream of history. Just as the influential English statesman, historian, and essayist Thomas Babington Macaulay (1800–1859) saw all of pre-Victorian history as leading inexorably to the ascension of the Whig Party (see his *History of England from the Accession of James II*), so do the majority of post-Enlightenment scholars see European history as evolving, step by grueling step, toward the triumph of secular institutions, rational science, and the autonomous individual. As long as we leave that interpretation unquestioned, we will have little success in restoring the Christian worldview to its rightful place in the public educational sphere. In the same way, Lewis, until he boldly proclaimed that the Renaissance had never happened, could not fully reclaim the great thinkers of the Renaissance as culminations of a vital Christian humanist strain dating back to the medieval and classical periods, rather than as proto–secular modernists who were stifled from speaking their mind by an oppressive church.

CHAPTER 21:

DINOSAURS IN THE CLASSROOM

T his leads in turn to the third thing Lewis can teach us: the need for Christian educators to immerse themselves in the life and spirit of premodern Europe. We may succeed in rehabilitating the past from its detractors and even in championing the role played by those past ages, but if we ourselves cannot sympathize and identify with the ages we are defending, then all our work will have been in vain. To defend the past merely as a thing to be studied is like defending Christian doctrine as nothing but a set of rational propositions. To do either is to capitulate, whether we realize it or not, to one of the core elements of the modernist worldview: namely, that the only things to be taken seriously, *really* seriously, are those things that can be observed, calculated, and outlined. In modern academia, the past is something to be studied and dissected, not something to be known and appreciated. Modern critics no longer learn at the feet of the great bards and philosophers of the past; more often than not, it is *they* who stand on the dais, looking with scorn (or at least suspicion) on the writers of the canon.

Not so Lewis, for whom premodern Europe (and especially the

Middle Ages) was a place he knew and loved intimately. As he explains it to his scholarly Cambridge audience in "De Descriptione Temporum":

> I myself belong far more to that Old Western order than to yours. I am going to claim that this, which in one way is a disqualification for my task, is yet in another a qualification. The disqualification is obvious. You don't want to be lectured on Neanderthal Man by a Neanderthal, still less on dinosaurs by a dinosaur. And yet, is that the whole story? If a live dinosaur dragged its slow length into the laboratory, would we not all look back as we fled? What a chance to know at last how it really moved and looked and smelled and what noises it made! . . . It is my settled conviction that in order to read Old Western literature aright you must suspend most of the responses and unlearn most of the habits you have acquired in reading modern literature. And because this is the judgment of a native, I claim that, even if the defense of my conviction is weak, the fact of my conviction is a historical *datum* to which you should give full weight. That way, where I fail as a critic, I may yet be useful as a specimen. I would even dare to go further. Speaking not only for myself but for all other Old Western men whom you may meet, I would say, use your specimens while you can. There are not going to be many more dinosaurs.

As a scholar, Lewis had a full and rich understanding of the medieval world, but as a man, he had something more: he was one who believed, embodied, and felt in his bones the moral and aesthetic values of Old Western culture. He knew what it meant to look upon the cosmos not as our house but as our home. He knew what it felt like to live in a meaningful, sympathetic universe, one in which nature was not a textbook to be studied, but a poem to be marveled at. He understood, "firsthand" as it were, how hierarchy could uplift and define rather than crush and limit, how religion could be the glue that held society together rather than the cause of division, how the classical virtues of prudence, justice, temperance, and courage and the theological virtues of faith, hope, and love could lie at the core of sociopolitical-clerical rule rather than the dictates of realpolitik.

In this Lewis was special, but he need not be unique. There are many of us Christian educators out there who could become dinosaurs ourselves if we would only spend the requisite time reading, relishing, and *absorbing* the great works of the past. We must open ourselves to what another modern Christian educator, T. S. Eliot, called the mind of the past; we must let the tradition sink in past those watchful dragons that would devour anything that smells even faintly of hierarchy, elitism, clericalism, or superstition. The best place to start, of course, is with Dante and Chaucer; to this, add Boethius, Augustine, St. Francis, and Aquinas, and you will be off to a great start. But again, don't just read, absorb: enter into the lives of the authors, and teach your students to do the same. Extend to the medievals the same sympathetic imagination that you would give to a reading or viewing of *The Lord of the Rings*. And as you read, remember one vital thing about Old Europe: premodern writers were *not* hung up about being original. They saw their task as that of carrying on a tradition that was much older than themselves and that would continue on long after they were dead.

You might also remember this sage advice from one of C. S. Lewis's closest friends, Charles Williams. In chapter 8 of *The Figure of Beatrice*, Williams informs us that Dante, being a good medieval, "believed it to be less important that men should think for themselves than that they should think rightly." When we read the medievals, we do not encounter men for whom self-expression was the be-all and end-all of art. We encounter instead men who believed that truth existed and who sought in their art and in their lives to approximate that truth.

CHAPTER 22:

GENIAL CRITICISM

W hat we need, in short, if we are to encounter the medievals on their own terms, is to learn and to read in a whole new way. Here too, I am happy to report, Lewis can be a most trusted guide. For the good professor, in his critiques not only of ages but also of individual works and genres, practiced supremely what I like to call (after Coleridge) *genial criticism*. Those wishing to see Lewis's genial criticism both explained and put into action will want to consult not only *The Allegory of Love*, *A Preface to Paradise Lost*, and *The Discarded Image*, but also two book-length essays he wrote early and late in his career, *The Personal Heresy* and *An Experiment in Criticism*, and the essays anthologized in *Selected Literary Essays* and *On Stories*. Lewis's work in this area is wide and varied and is undergirded by much reflection on what constitutes fair criticism; still, its essence can be conveyed in four practical rules of thumb:

1. Critics who dislike a certain genre should not judge works in that genre.
2. Works must be interpreted in a way that is true to the values of its author/age.

3. Focus should remain on the work itself and not the author of the work.

4. Critics should seek first to learn from (rather than judge) the canon.

Were modern educators to adopt these four simple principles and put them into practice, I think it would revolutionize not only our academies but our primary and secondary schools as well. Let us, therefore, consider each of them carefully.

1. In what should be considered one of his seminal essays, "On Science Fiction," anthologized in both *On Stories* and *Of Other Worlds*, Lewis lays down a critical framework for analyzing and assessing this often misunderstood genre. Though the reputation of science fiction has risen over the last several decades, when Lewis wrote his essay in 1955, little academic or critical attention had been paid to the genre, and what little it had received was generally negative. In his essay, Lewis perceptively identifies the source of this negativity as residing less in the works themselves than in the personal prejudices of the critics. Like "ungenial" film critics who pan a comedy not because the film under review is intrinsically bad but because they despise *all* film comedies, many of the negative reviews of science-fiction novels rested on a refusal to take the *genre* seriously rather than on any objective critical standards. Reflecting on this phenomenon, Lewis argues that such reviews

> are useless because, while purporting to condemn the book, they only reveal the reviewer's dislike of the kind to which it belongs. Let bad tragedies be censured by those who love tragedy, and bad detective stories by those who love the detective story. Then we shall learn their real faults. Otherwise we shall find epics blamed for not being novels, farces for not being high comedies, novels by James for lacking the swift action of Smollett. Who wants to hear a particular claret abused by a fanatical teetotaler, or a particular woman by a confirmed misogynist?

In keeping with this sage advice, Lewis goes on in the rest of his essay to establish criteria by which science fiction can be assessed on its own merits and in accordance with its own set conventions and proper ends.

Though the specifics of Lewis's analysis do not here concern us, his overall approach is one from which we can all benefit. Indeed, whether we realize it or not, his approach *has* benefited us, since Lewis (along with J. R. R. Tolkien) is largely responsible for rehabilitating the reputation of fairy tales and "children's" literature in general, which had been held in high regard during the nineteenth century, but which had fallen into disrepute during the first half of the twentieth. Christians have long been accused (usually unfairly, but in many cases justly) for being naysayers who are suspicious of the arts and unwilling to appreciate or celebrate them. Would it not be a wonderful witness to the world if Christian teachers of all kinds were to be seen in a new light: as upholders and defenders of the arts in all their varied genres? We attack (in many cases rightly) the decadence of the arts, but we offer nothing in their place, no other genres that can wrestle honestly and effectively with the key issues of our modern world.

Serendipitously, the turn of the century provided us with a possible way of doing so. Around the year 2000, various independent surveys of the British reading public found that those polled overwhelmingly voted *The Lord of the Rings* as the best book of the century. Rather than support these findings, the British literati mounted a scathing attack both on the voters and on their choice, vehemently rejecting any literary merit to Tolkien's masterpiece. (For a full and powerful survey of this revealing phenomenon, see *Tolkien: Man and Myth* by Joseph Pearce.) Needless to say, most of these attacks rested not on a close assessment of the work's flaws but on the critics' severe dislike for the genre of epic fantasy. To these self-appointed watchmen of aesthetic taste, Tolkien was nothing more than a purveyor of bourgeois escapism, unworthy to be mentioned in the same breath with "serious" authors like Joyce or Lawrence or Nabokov. In the face of such an assault, the onus rests on every Christian educator who has ever read and loved *The Lord of the Rings* to mount a defense, not just of the book itself but of the genre to which it belongs. And that defense (which has already begun to be mounted) must not only identify and celebrate the Christian worldview that underlies the epic, but also define and describe both the conventions of the genre and the methods by which Tolkien uses these conventions to comment on contemporary and perennial problems.

2. That is to say, we must do for *The Lord of the Rings* what Lewis did for *Paradise Lost*. Just as critics today willfully ignore the full scope and import of Tolkien's epic vision, so critics since 1800 have increasingly refused to read and interpret Milton's epic in a way that does justice to Milton's beliefs and the conventions of the genre he chose. Rather than attempt to read and experience the epic from Milton's point of view (or the point of view of his original readers), we impose on the work our own modern skepticism and our own reordering of the classical and Christian virtues. Lewis writes in chapter 9 of *A Preface to Paradise Lost*, "Milton's thought, when purged of its theology, does not exist." And yet, that is exactly what post-Enlightenment criticism has done to Milton. We would make a protomodern of him, rather than challenging ourselves to see the world from the eyes of one to whom the Christian story of creation and fall was more than a mere myth. In the same chapter, Lewis offers an antidote for this distinctly ungenial criticism:

> Instead of stripping the knight of his armor you can try to put his armor on yourself; instead of seeing how the courtier would look without his lace, you can try to see how you would feel with his lace; that is, with his honor, his wit, his royalism, and his gallantries out of the Grand Cyrus. I had much rather know what I should feel like if I adopted the beliefs of Lucretius than how Lucretius would have felt if he had never entertained them. The possible Lucretius in myself interests me more than the possible C. S. Lewis in Lucretius. . . . You must, so far as in you lies, become an Achaean chief while reading Homer, a medieval knight while reading Malory, and an eighteenth century Londoner while reading Johnson. Only thus will you be able to judge the work "in the same spirit that its author writ" and to avoid chimerical criticism.

It is refreshing that Lewis here uses Lucretius as an example of an ancient writer to whom we must extend our sympathetic imagination if we are to appreciate fully his work: refreshing, I say, because Lucretius's worldview was antithetical to that of the Christian Lewis. As a genial critic, Professor Lewis was able to grant the Epicurean Lucretius the same "willing suspension of disbelief" that he expected naturalist critics to grant to the supernaturalist Milton.

As Christian educators we must work hard to instill this kind of sensibility in our students. We must teach them not to force all works to fit the concerns and "hang-ups" of our own day and age, but to immerse themselves in the culture and belief system that produced the work. Of course, if they really learn to do this, they will quickly find that the work will repay them by giving them a new perspective *on* their concerns and hang-ups. Then they will discover, to paraphrase Eliot again, that all ages are ever contemporaneous with our own, that the truly vital questions do not change.

3. The advice Lewis gives in *A Preface to Paradise Lost* may seem, at first, to stand in stark contrast to his insistence in *The Personal Heresy* and elsewhere that we avoid any type of biographical criticism that would interpret a work through the lens of its author's life. But the contradiction is more apparent than real. To define carefully the conventions and worldview that underlie a work of literature and to lose oneself in the inner workings of the characters who populate it are but two ways of assessing the work on its own terms. Such an approach is radically different from that of post-Freudian critics who would reduce the work to an aesthetic sublimation of the phobias, complexes, and/or neuroses of its creator. As long as we fix our gaze on the author, we will never see the work for what it is in itself; indeed, we risk seeing it merely as a product of individual self-expression, rather than a repository of truths and beauties that transcend the experiences and struggles of the author.

Interestingly, in arguing against criticism that interprets a literary work solely as the highly personal self-expression of an author, Lewis (perhaps inadvertently) paralleled the work of the American New Critics, most of whom were traditional Southerners who espoused a Christian worldview (if not always a fixed belief in the creeds themselves). Two of these New Critics, W. K. Wimsatt and Monroe C. Beardsley, spoke out against what they dubbed the "intentional fallacy": the critical temptation to judge poems solely on the basis of what the poet intended. By counseling their students to resist this temptation, neither Wimsatt nor Beardsley meant to advocate a relativistic approach to interpretation or a nihilistic approach to meaning. For them (as for Lewis) works *did* have a meaning, but that meaning inhered in the work itself and not in some abstract intention floating around in the author's mind. For the poem (or novel) is finally more real and concrete than the poet's (or novelist's) intention; to place all our focus on the latter is to nudge criticism into an abstract realm where meaning can easily slip away, only to be replaced by the agendas and prejudices of the critic.

4. And when *that* happens, *both* the poet and his work are dethroned, and the critic instead reigns supreme. Just as a liberal theologian may be defined as someone who judges the Bible rather than letting the Bible judge him, so the ungenial critic is finally someone who views the works of the canon (and their authors) not as tutors to be learned from but unruly children to be taught. It is perhaps true that there have been times when educators and students have suffered from an excess of "bardolatry." If so, it is not an affliction from which our age suffers. Indeed, our age desperately needs a resurgence of respect (and even awe) for the great writers and works of the Western tradition. We must learn again to sit at the feet of Homer and Dante and Shakespeare and to experience that shiver of joy and fear that one feels in the presence of one's first love. Rather than attempt to pigeonhole the great poets or to accuse them of holding beliefs that we now consider illiberal or politically incorrect, we need to test our own beliefs against the touchstone of their timeless works. It is this method, this practice, this attitude of critical humility that we must instill in our students.

And in ourselves.

CHAPTER 23:

THE HISTORICAL
POINT OF VIEW

P erhaps C. S. Lewis's single greatest comment on the dangers of modern criticism appears not in any of his scholarly books or essays but in what is surely his most popular work of apologetics: *The Screwtape Letters*. In this most delightful and most disturbing of books, Lewis provides us with a series of thirty-one letters sent from a senior devil named Screwtape to his nephew, Wormwood, for the purpose of instructing the young devil in the fine art of temptation. The letters, though timeless in their content and exact in their satanic voicing, are nevertheless quickly recognizable as the work of C. S. Lewis. For Lewis, more than any other twentieth-century Christian writer, saw clearly how Satan seeks to destroy not only our faith and our virtue, but our reason as well. As Screwtape carefully explains to Wormwood in his letters, humans are easier to tempt and seduce when they are kept in a perpetual state of hazy, imprecise abstraction. Despite the fact that atheists nearly always point to reason as the bedrock of their atheism, clear, rational thinking, when it is carried out to its logical and proper end, always leads back to the One who created human reason in the first place and who gave it to us as a gift. "No," Screwtape advises his nephew, "best to breed in his human 'patient' an excess of sloppy thinking."

Indeed, the safest method of all is to cut him off from any set standards of reason or ethics by which he might be tempted to judge his ideas as being true or false, moral or immoral. Isolate him from any form of truth or beauty that is greater than he is, and you leave him naked and unprotected. As such, one of the greatest enemies of Satan is—dare I say it—the traditional liberal-arts teacher: the one, that is, who exposes his students to the great works of the past. Satan is by no means a clever or creative being. He's been assaulting our fallen human race with the same basic lies, snares, and temptations for thousands of years. The Great Books that make up the Western canon all document, in their own way, the ongoing human struggle to seek virtue and avoid vice. To enable and empower students to wrestle with these books and to discern their truth claims is to equip them to see through many of the drearily repetitive lies of Satan. It helps them (and, by extension, the human race to which they belong) to break out of that vicious cycle of sin and ignorance in which the Devil seeks to trap us, our ancestors, and our heirs.

Yes, a full knowledge of and wrestling with the Great Books (what has, until recently, formed the core of true education) offers one of the best humanistic means to guard against the lies of the Enemy. Such an education cannot, of course, save us or our students from sin itself: only Christ can do that, and only the Bible is fully reliable on matters of salvation. Still, just as Human Reason, in the guise of Virgil, proves a most helpful guide to Dante and paves the way for the coming of the fuller revelation of Divine Grace, in Beatrice, so can the Great Books (properly taught and understood) lead us along the right path.

Or so they could in the past. According to Screwtape's twenty-seventh letter, the ever-wakeful propaganda departments of hell have found a way to counter this influence:

> Only the learned read old books, and we have now so dealt with the learned that they are of all men the least likely to acquire wisdom by doing so. We have done this by inculcating the Historical Point of View. The Historical Point of View, put briefly, means that when a

learned man is presented with any statement in an ancient author, the one question he never asks is whether it is true. He asks who influenced the ancient writer, and how far the statement is consistent with what he said in other books, and what phase in the writer's development, or in the general history of thought, it illustrates, and how it affected later writers, and how often it has been misunderstood (specially by the learned man's own colleagues) and what the general course of criticism on it has been for the last ten years, and what is the "present state of the question." To regard the ancient writer as a possible source of knowledge—to anticipate that what he said could possibly modify your thoughts or your behaviour—this would be rejected as unutterably simple-minded. And since we cannot deceive the whole human race all the time, it is most important thus to cut every generation off from all others; for where learning makes a free commerce between the ages there is always the danger that the characteristic errors of one may be corrected by the characteristic truths of another. But, thanks be to Our Father and the Historical Point of View, great scholars are now as little nourished by the past as the most ignorant mechanic who holds that "history is bunk."

I wish, as a professor myself, that I could dismiss the above paragraph as a gross exaggeration, but I cannot. Lewis is dead-on in his satirical exposé of the academy. Read almost any modern scholarly critique of the classics, and you will find that the issue of whether the truth claims made in the work are in fact true will *never* be raised. This is just as much the case when the work being considered is philosophical or theological, as when it is lyrical or dramatic. That the scholar, or those who read his work, might actually learn something from the classic under discussion (or, God forbid, modify their beliefs or actions on the basis of that learning) is not just irrelevant; it is beneath consideration.

As Christian educators (at whatever level), we must do all in our power to counter this trend toward studying the past solely as an end in itself, rather than as a means of striving toward higher truths and greater beauty. We must, in short, read and teach the "old books" and "ancient authors" in conjunction with the great questions: Who am I? Why am I here? What is my purpose? We must train our students to determine what each Great Book can teach us about the nature of the good man, the good life, and the good society. And once they *do* determine that, we must encourage them to *act* on what they have found: to shape their lives, their goals, and their decisions against the books they read as a carpenter shapes a piece of wood against a lathe.

CHAPTER 24:

THE PROFESSOR AS
PUBLIC EDUCATOR

A s educators, we must work hard to draw our students into the Great Dialogue that has been going on since Homer and the Bible. But we must not stop there. We must not be content to allow knowledge to remain walled up in the "ivory tower" of the academy. Those of us (and here I am speaking specifically to my fellow university professors) who have been gifted with the time and opportunity to devote nine or more years of our lives to studying and absorbing the Great Books must be willing to share what we have learned with people inside and outside our classroom. We would think it a strange (indeed, unseemly) thing if a pastor preached from his pulpit with power and truth every Sunday morning but then refused to interpret the Scriptures to a soul-hungry man whom he met on the bus or in a plane. And yet, are not we whose vocation it is to educate others guilty of the same thing when we confine our teaching to an academic setting alone?

As is well known, Lewis never received a professorship at Oxford, despite the adulation of his students and the fame of his many books. Most Christians who learn this sad fact immediately assume that the underlying reason for this was Lewis's outspoken Christian faith. This, of course, *was* a key factor in his failure to receive the promotion and title he so richly deserved, but it was not the only factor. The academic prejudice (and even animosity) that prevented Lewis from receiving a professorship was based not just on his "politically incorrect" beliefs but also on the fact that he dared to write popular books for a popular audience. How dare an Oxford don consort with the rabble and write books in language simple enough for them to understand. How dare he insult the dignity of Oxford by writing of philosophical, theological, and aesthetic matters in such "dumbed-down" terms. Of course, anyone who has read Lewis's works will know that they are anything but dumbed down, but it is true that they are written in a manner refreshingly free from all academic pretension and scholarly jargon. And they are wonderfully, blissfully free of footnotes!

In stark contrast to most of his colleagues, who (in keeping with the scientific spirit of the age) often adopted an impersonal, "objective" tone in their work, Lewis was unafraid to write in a warm, engaging first person that mimicked, in many ways, the personal, conversational style of G. K. Chesterton. He wrote not like a specialized scholar who misses the forest for the trees but like a true generalist who saw trees and forest together. He was, in short, less a "scholarly writer" than what used to be called a man of letters. As such, his true peers are not to be found in the modern university, but among those great essayists of the Victorian Age (Cardinal Newman, John Ruskin, Thomas Carlyle, Matthew Arnold, etc.) who engaged and challenged the public with their work. Indeed, in a sad irony, the modern reader will find more of Lewis's spirit in the secular humanist *New York Review of Books* than in faith-based journals such as *Christianity and Literature*.

Of course, that does not mean that the voice of the Christian man of letters has disappeared. Magazines like *Touchstone*, *First Things*, and *The City* are still keeping it alive, but it has become rarer among university professors. Since Lewis's day, the work coming out of the academy (whether secular or Christian) has grown increasingly jargoned, obscure, and elitist. Indeed, in another sad irony, it is precisely those professors who champion liberal, socially conscious causes (meant to empower the people) that produce the most elitist work of all: work that other Ph.D.s often have a hard time understanding!

Let us, like Lewis, have the courage to step out of our academic robes and enter the public arena, not as pontificators or know-it-alls or stuffed shirts, but as lovers alive with passion for the things we teach. Let us celebrate, along with Lewis, the beauty, wonder, and truth that run rampant through those Great Books of which we are (whether we like it or not) the guardians, executors, and midwives. Let us not hoard the treasures that have been entrusted to us, but let us freely and enthusiastically disseminate them to all those who have ears to hear.

CHAPTER 25:

RESTORING VIRTUE

T he modern educator who successfully integrated into his teaching and scholarship the advice laid out in only three of the preceding six chapters would have gone a long way toward living up to the legacy of Lewis the Oxford and Cambridge don. Still, even if he were able to carry out the advice in all six chapters, one thing necessary would yet be lacking: one final task that, if left undone, could render the preceding six null and void. I speak of a task that should lie (and has tradition-ally lain) at the center of education: namely, the instilling of virtue. As Lewis so prophetically reveals in *The Abolition of Man*, public education in the West has (since the Enlightenment) progressively abandoned its duty to instruct the young in the ways of virtue. Worse yet, our schools have ceased to forge the necessary link between these virtues (and their corresponding vices) and the proper emotional reaction that they should provoke in those who engage in virtuous/vicious behavior. Indeed, rather than train students to feel a swell of pride when they read a patriotic poem or listen to "The Star-Spangled Banner," we actually ridicule the whole notion of patriotism as sentimental at best and suspect at worst. Rather than nurture in our young men a sense of chivalry and a desire to treat women with respect and courtesy, we encourage them to objectify and demythologize women, to view them as nothing more than men with breasts. Rather than inspire in them a feeling of reverential fear or romantic love when they come into the presence of that which is sublime or beautiful, we emasculate sublimity, deconstruct beauty, and belittle anyone who might be "taken in" by them.

The purported goal of this disillusionment is to ready children, teens, and/or young adults for the "real" world, to open their eyes to how things "really" work. The Great Books are fine as educational tools, but let us not encourage our students to "buy in" to the narrow, premodern, illiberal notions of virtue and vice that they espouse. Let us not, for goodness' sake, allow them to fall back into rank sentimentalism at the very moment our civilization is charging forward into a utopia of scientism and rationalism. You see, explains Lewis in chapter 1 of *The Abolition of Man*, modern educators, afraid that their charges will be "swayed by emotional propaganda . . . conclude that the best thing they can do is to fortify the minds of young people against emotion." In response to this sincere but misguided goal, Lewis offers his own incisive critique:

> My own experience as a teacher tells an opposite tale. For every one pupil who needs to be guarded from a weak excess of sensibility there are three who need to be awakened from the slumber of cold vulgarity. The task of the modern educator is not to cut down jungles but to irrigate deserts. The right defense against false sentiments is to inculcate just sentiments. By starving the sensibility of our pupils we only make them easier prey to the propagandist when he comes. For famished nature will be avenged and a hard heart is no infallible protection against a soft head.

As any gardener will tell you, the best defense against weeds is not more weed killer but stronger, healthier grass. What our young people need if they are to survive in this world is not to have their "eyes opened" but their hearts and souls strengthened. By stripping away from them not only the classical and Judeo-Christian virtues on which Western civilization was built, but also the proper emotions that those virtues should inspire, we leave them vulnerable to every new "ism" that comes along. Apart from a firm grounding in virtue (felt equally strong in the mind and in the gut), people of *whatever* age are apt to fall for any new con man peddling a new morality.

No, if we are to truly protect our students from the dangers of the modern world, then we need to revive in them what Lewis (in chapter 8 of *A Preface to Paradise Lost*) calls stock responses. Paraphrasing the twentieth-century American literary critic I. A. Richards, Lewis defines a stock response as "a deliberately organized attitude which is substituted for 'the direct free play of experience.'" While agreeing in principle with Richards's definition, Lewis puts his own unique twist on it:

> In my opinion such deliberate organization is one of the first necessities of human life, and one of the main functions of art is to assist it. All that we describe as constancy in love or friendship, as loyalty in political life, or, in general, as perseverance—all solid virtue and stable pleasure—depends on organizing chosen attitudes and maintaining them against the eternal flux (or "direct free play") of mere immediate experience. This Dr. Richards would not perhaps deny. But his school puts the emphasis the other way. They talk as if improvement of our responses were always required in the direction of finer discrimination and greater particularity; never as if men needed responses more normal and more traditional than they now have. To me, on the other hand, it seem that most people's responses are not "stock" enough, and that the play of experience is too free and too direct in most of us for safety or happiness or human dignity.

Living as we do in a posthippie world that condemns insincerity as the worst of all sins, we may at first react negatively to this passage. Lewis's defense of stock responses may sound to us like a call to stifle our "natural" emotions and put on a societal mask. It is not. What Lewis (after Plato and Aristotle, Aquinas and Dante) calls for is not the warping or falsifying of our emotional responses but the proper ordering of our desires. Apart from such an ordering, communal life quickly regresses into barbarism, and the individual is left a prey to his own base lusts. Stock responses are the great safeguards of "happiness [and] human dignity"; in their absence, life becomes, to quote English philosopher Thomas Hobbes (1588–1679), somewhat against him, "nasty, brutish, and short."

In his dystopic novel, *That Hideous Strength*, Lewis's male protagonist, Mark Studdock, is seduced into joining an evil organization bent on seizing control of England and converting it into a "scientific" totalitarian state run by themselves. Had Mark's stock responses to virtue and vice been stronger, he would never have been so easily fooled by their propaganda and their veneer of humanitarian concern and academic respectability. At the climax of Mark's journey into the darkness of ethical relativism and spiritual disharmony (chapter 14), he is thrown by his seducers into a lopsided room meant to detach him finally and fully from all standards of truth, virtue, and beauty. In one sense, the lopsided room is meant to represent a sort of anticlassroom in which students are taught to call black white and white black. In another sense, it is meant to be a metaphor for a type of modernist classroom that actually does exist and that encourages its students to abandon both the traditional distinction between virtue and vice and the traditional emotional responses that should accompany them.

In the end, Mark is saved from the existential and nihilistic despair that the lopsided room embodies by divine intervention and by the sudden resurgence within him of a sense of that which is normal. May we as Christian educators never forget that one of our greatest duties is to produce and nurture within our students just such a sense of normalcy. Proverbs 22:6 promises us that if we "train up a child in the way he should go . . . when he is old, he will not depart from it." The same truth holds true today, whether that child be a fifth grader, a high school junior, or a college freshman. We must rehabilitate and revive the virtues of the past for them, not so that they can stand in superior judgment over those virtues, but so that they can learn from them. Just so, we must steer our students into an encounter and a wrestling with the Great Books, not so that they will become effete elitists cut off from the "people," but so that they will learn to see themselves as participants in a noble tradition: in a higher kind of normalcy that affirms that which is most human and most perennial.

EPILOGUE

KNOW THY ENEMY

SCREWTAPE'S
MILLENNIAL TOAST

(The date is December 31, 2000; the place is a posh hotel conference room in an upper-income region of hell. The League of Senior Tempters has gathered to toast in the new millennium, and they have invited as their guest speaker a legendary tempter and trainer of young devils: Screwtape. After the usual formalities, Screwtape begins his address.)

I thank you for giving me the opportunity to address you tonight. For forty years now I have been engaged in a massive project that has demanded unprecedented cooperation between the various branches of the Ministry of Temptation and that has consumed untold resources and devil hours. Even our Father Below has taken an active role in what has proved to be our greatest undertaking since the Crusades. What, you may be asking yourselves, is this new scourge of which I speak? Another world war perhaps, a second Enlightenment, a renewed attempt to fool the humans into thinking they can build utopia? For shame, gentledevils. Do you think we in hell have completely lost our imagination? Don't believe those lies of the Enemy that say we in hell can only pervert and destroy. Even now we have succeeded in stealing from the Enemy what he has long claimed to be his prerogative alone: the creation of a new species of man. Ah yes, laugh if you will, but we have done it, done it so well that the humans have yet to recognize this new species rising up in their midst. Why do you look so dumbfounded, my fellow tempters? Have you too been fooled? Allow me then to rip the veil from your eyes that you may know this species and learn how best to tempt it. Let us explore together the habits, rituals, and unique life cycle of the American teenager.

For some time, I must admit, I was frightened. It looked as if postwar prosperity in America would play right into the Enemy's hands. Think of it: millions of young Americans freed from backbreaking toil, allowed the time and opportunity to nurture their imagination and their fledgling sense of wonder. Imagine, if you can stomach it, an army of boys and girls reading those horrid plays and novels and poems that the Enemy so loves. Picture them dialoguing as equals with these dead scribblers (please, Liposuk, if you're going to be sick, do leave the room) and, horror of horrors, adding their own unique contributions to the cesspool of human creativity. Just think how the Enemy could have used those desires to direct all those impressionable young scholars to himself. Yes, my gentledevils, for several years the situation looked grim indeed.

But do not worry; we rallied immediately and met the danger head-on. We knew we could do nothing to eliminate their newfound leisure time, so we shifted our tactics. Instead of trying to foment a new outbreak of child labor (ah, the good old days; how I loved to watch those little porkers sweat), we simply filled up their leisure with an endless flow of mindless and mind-numbing trash.

As most of you are well aware, the Clamor & Bedlam section of hell has long been trying to find new ways to drown out that awful music of the spheres that the Enemy has been assaulting our ears with for the last ten thousand years. And if that were not torture enough, the Enemy insists on producing new human composers every generation to echo those celestial harmonies on earth. If I have to hear that Air on the G String one more time, I think I will rip out my own ears! Selfish tyrant that he is, he even stole from us the common herd. Into their dull, pathetic lives, he brought folk music and opera and brass bands. He gave them musical shows and sickening waltzes and those blasted tunes of Gershwin, Porter, and Rodgers that I still can't beat out of my brain.

Yes, the struggle has been a difficult one, but we have finally prevailed. For five hundred years the forges of hell huffed and groaned, until, but a mere fifty years ago, they spat out their greatest invention: an infernal machine with the power to demolish every melody the Enemy ever conceived. The humans call it an electric guitar, but we in hell call it by its real name: the Din-maker. True, a few tricky humans have succeeded in coaxing occasional moments of joy from the Din-maker, but they are few and far between. Fueled by our success with the Din-maker, we next took their drums, which the Enemy had given them to help keep time, and turned them into, of all things, melodic instruments. My fellow tempters, you simply *must* listen to what the humans now call rap, hip-hop, and heavy metal; our own C & B band would be hard pressed to produce music of such undiluted ugliness and cacophony. It's simply wonderful; no human could possibly harbor an intelligent or passionate or spiritual thought while listening to the stuff. But there's more! Over the last century, even those beloved composers of the Enemy have begun to embrace this same hell-born ugliness and cacophony; they call it atonal music, but we in hell call *it* too by its real name: Noise. Lovely, lovely Noise. Tearing down every higher spiritual thought the humans ever had, disconnecting them from all celestial harmony, perverting that most terrible gift of the Enemy (the sense of beauty). How foolish the Enemy was to make such a firm link between Truth and Beauty. Did he not know we would first demolish Beauty and then leave Truth to atrophy?

I can see by your faces that many of you think I have digressed, but I have not. I told you a moment ago that our new strategy for distracting the American youth from any form of intellectual or spiritual growth was to fill his leisure time with trash. Well, gentledevils, the degradation of their popular music (not to mention the barbaric and grotesque dancing that accompanies it) has been for many years now our first line of defense. You simply cannot imagine how much of their time and energy the American youth (from here on in I shall call him by his species name: teenager) pours into rap, heavy metal, and their many derivatives. Those delicious humans have even invented (without our help, mind you) a machine that allows the teenager to strap his music to his ears and carry it with him wherever he goes. It has proved an absolute boon in ensuring that the teen suffers no interruption from an unending stream of Noise. Believe me, my fellow tempters, there is no more effective way to block messages from the Enemy; one might as well try to discern a whisper in the midst of a pack of braying donkeys.

In many cases, the music has spurred the teens on to violence. This, of course, is a good thing and very helpful to our cause, but don't be led astray by these random outbreaks. The real purpose of the music is to make them numb, to incapacitate them for real human feeling and fellowship. We gave it to them not that they might have fun (emptiness not happiness is what we seek), but so that they might become desensitized to that terrible beauty, wonder, and mystery the Enemy has spread so liberally among them. That accursed Creator! He can use the smallest flower, the most pathetic animal to grab a hold of their hearts and draw them upward to his presence. It pains me to admit it, but the Enemy has even converted some of them to his cause through musicians who play our own infernal music on our own drums and Din-makers. How, how can we fight an Enemy who can use anything, simply anything as a means to recruit humans? You'll no doubt remember that time when the Enemy used a donkey to trick one of our own prophets. It's simply disgusting and decidedly unfair.

Still, we mustn't despair. The music has been far more effective for our cause than his. Even those whom he *does* win to his side can usually be held in a state of spiritual torpor by heavy doses of the music. And besides, it has so many other uses! Not only does it isolate and divide them from their parents and teachers; it severs them from history and from reality itself. The concerts are a truly beautiful thing (how I've enjoyed the deafening Noise, the bestial gyrations, the loss of individual dignity), but beware that camaraderie does not break out. Your focus must remain firmly on using the music to provide the teen with an illusionary, "masturbational" world safe from adult supervision. In this area, I would suggest heavy use of what has proved to be the crown of our Teenage Corruption Project (TCP): the music video. If you think rap and heavy metal are effective soul crushers, wait till you see what happens when the music is wedded to a kaleidoscope of violent and sexual images that flash on the retina at dizzying speed! Let the Enemy try his best; I defy him to work his redemptive magic on these wonderful products of the infernal imagination.

But wait, the usefulness of the music does not stop here. The inbred tendency on the part of young people to model themselves after heroes and leaders has generally worked in the Enemy's favor, but not anymore. The modern teenager actually idolizes the creators of this music; indeed, they often follow them like sheep, ascribing to them the respect and authority once reserved for their own fathers. Focus your best efforts on the rock star, and, along with him, you will drag in a whole pack of adoring fans. And believe me, my fellow tempters, this is not a hard task. Their heavy use of drugs, their belief in the absolute goodness and sanctity of their own self-expression, and their generally warped appetites and desires make these teen idols prime candidates for demonic control.

But a word of warning. Once you have roped in the rock star and you watch the teens begin to gather around him, you must make sure to whisper into each of their ears that their idolatry of the musician is an expression of their own individual choices and tastes rather than what it truly is: a herd instinct. Encourage them to think (and believe) that while their churchgoing friends are all dreary copies of one another, they are unique, special, an elite corps of free individuals who have risen above the common mass of humanity. By no means let them see that they and all their fellow fans look and dress and act exactly alike. Remember, self-deception is our greatest tool for separating them from the will and the grace of the Enemy. The more they efface their true identity, the more you must convince them that they have freed themselves from all bourgeois standards and restrictions. The more they surrender their will to us, the more you must puff them up with a belief in their own triumphant will to power.

Here, of course, Nietzsche is most helpful. (Ah, Nietzsche, Nietzsche, how fondly I remember *that* soul; even as I devoured it, it kept denying my existence.) Fill your teen charges to the brim with Nietzsche's argument that all religion is a slave ethic and that they must move themselves beyond middle-class notions of good and evil. But, whatever you do, do not allow them to read Nietzsche himself. Their understanding of Nietzsche's philosophy must lead always to a simple, mindless nihilism: to a belief that everything is relative and that there are no objective moral or theological absolutes. Remember, though Nietzsche is one of our greatest allies, there are still in his works dangerous ideas. Nietzsche has an annoying habit of uncovering hypocrisies that we would rather keep hidden and of inspiring a kind of individual growth and maturity that poses a major threat to our overall plan for the modern world. And that plan is simply this: to fashion a lowest-common-denominator world where all true creativity is crushed and any attempt to rise above mediocrity is attacked as elitist and undemocratic.

In my last public address (before devoting my full time to the Teenage Corruption Project), I advised the young devils of the Tempter's Training College to foster at all costs a diabolical version of the democratic ethos. I dubbed that diabolic ethos "the spirit of I'm as good as you," and, if I may so pride myself on my prophetic powers, you will note that nearly every public educational initiative in America has helped realize our goal of producing a mass of young people who know nothing of their tradition or heritage but live trapped in a contemporary box of ideas from which most are unable to escape. Oh, what a joy it is to watch young minds be stifled in the name of political correctness or multiculturalism or all those other wonderful euphemisms the humans come up with to justify their rabid envy of true intelligence and creativity. If they were really allowed to read and enjoy Plato or Augustine or Dante, the teens would see through most of our temptations with ease; but never fear, this rarely happens in the modern America we have helped create. When any of these dangerous ideas do sneak through, we simply drown them out with the music, or, in those who cannot be so distracted, we insert into their minds a feeling of superiority over the tradition they barely understand.

Or there is another way, one that I am particularly fond of and that I (yes, I) helped develop. One day, while devouring the soul of Picasso, it struck me that the best defense against the various dangers posed by a knowledge of the tradition was a strong offense. Let me explain. Behind those "great" books that the Enemy so loves is not only an attempt to discern Truth but a reaching after and a celebration of Beauty (as I suggested a moment ago, the Enemy foolishly linked these concepts not only in his universe but also in the souls of the humans he created). I thought what better way to head off any appreciation of, or desire for, Beauty than to produce in the teen population a craving after ugliness. Impossible, you say! On the contrary, it is *very* possible. Indeed, it has been done. Throughout America (and Europe as well), girls whose physical beauty might have been used to celebrate the glory of the Creator have purposely and self-consciously "uglified" themselves. They shave off their hair or dye it with grotesque colors. They wear clothes that are drab, colorless, and formless. Even better, they (along with their male counterparts) pierce their bodies in a hundred different places. Not since the Gnostics of the early church have I seen such hatred of the physical body, such disgust for the human form (in both its masculinity and its femininity). They live, by their own choice, in a world of ugliness; their music, their art, their literature, their language, even their cartoons reinforce their degraded view of humanity and (the real goal, here) themselves.

True, their media people are continually assaulting the teens with images of beautiful women in movies, on TV, and on magazine covers. But the "beauty" of these women has little to do with what the Enemy calls Beauty; indeed, one might almost use the word *ugly* to describe them. Their figures are unnaturally thin, their features distorted, their expressions narcissistic. They have neither charm nor grace nor modesty, but a primitive and devouring aggressiveness that is finally more masculine than feminine. It was we, of course, who first taught their media people how to create and market this infernal beauty and who then taught the teens either to seek after it or to embrace instead the ugliness I just described. Either way, they end up severed from the Enemy's notion of Beauty. Either way, we win.

At this point, most of you may be asking yourselves how we have prevented the adult population from leading their teens out of this lowest-common-denominator world. Gentledevils, that is the best news of all! Since time began, young people have learned and grown by imitating the behavior and culture of their parents and other elders in the community. But today, through much labor and toil, we have succeeded in reversing this process. Though it seems impossible to believe, in American today the adults often pattern themselves after their own teenage children. When their teens play music that is physically painful to the ears, the adults do not attempt to instill in them a higher aesthetic taste or challenge their notion of what is beautiful. Rather, they wonder within themselves why *they* are unable to "understand" this music and endeavor to conform themselves to the tastes and lifestyles of their progeny. What long, wonderful hours of laughter I have had watching the pathetic attempts of grown men and women to adapt themselves to teen culture (now how's that for an infernal oxymoron!). Indeed, whereas most popular entertainment in America used to be directed at a mature audience, nearly all such entertainment has been degraded to the level of pubescent and even prepubescent children. Of course, this was part of our plan as well. We made sure to equip the American teen with an almost endless supply of excess cash, thus ensuring that every marketer and advertiser in the country would target them. With each passing year, their civilization, if I may coin a new word, becomes more and more "adolescentized." No longer are the arts made to embody lasting values or to rise above the prejudices of a given time and place; rather, they concentrate on short-lived shock value meant either to numb or to titillate, but by no means to inspire deep thought and contemplation of higher truths. Mediocrity is the rule, but it is a mediocrity that carries with it an urgency. It must be possessed *now*, no matter the cost.

For you see, teenagers, no matter the level and intensity of their rebellion against society, are first and foremost consumers. If they ever once question or doubt their role as consumer, be sure to whisper in their ear that it is only "fair" that they immediately have everything that their parents have. Make sure, of course, that the thought never once strikes them that their parents did not have these things until they were well into their thirties or even forties. Give them a lust for stuff on demand, and make them feel that it is their due, their inalienable right. And once you've established such impulsive behavior, let this too trickle upward to their parents. Let their parents feel that they too must have the newest cars, the fastest computers, the latest gadgets. Let them feel that without such things they are inadequate, perhaps even bad parents. Let discontent flow down like a mighty river, until all feelings of thankfulness have been eradicated. (By the way, did you notice how we've taught most of their media people to refer to Thanksgiving as Turkey Day?) And if you really want to have fun with the teenagers, convince them to despise all bourgeois standards as mean and hypocritical while simultaneously impelling them to purchase the most expensive stereo equipment available (paid for, of course, by their parents' credit card). Even more fun, teach them to upbraid their parents for being destroyers of the environment while hiding from them the glaring fact that theirs is the most disposable, fast-food, throw-away generation in history.

Such is the modern teenager, and, wonder of wonders, the Americans have so taken him to their hearts that they have packaged him, marketed him, and now export him to every country of the world. How it fills me with joy to watch the nations of the world ignorantly imitate every bad habit of America (I mean bad by the Enemy's standards, of course) while resisting those very virtues that we have long sought to stifle. The seed we planted in America has indeed born fruit; the world is quickly being united not (as the deluded politicians think) by real respect for the dignity of man, but by infernal music videos, adolescent Hollywood films, and a lust for unrestrained consumerism.

My fellow tempters, I wish that I could end my speech here with a claim of absolute victory, but alas, the modern teenager has within him certain unique qualities that the Enemy has often used to pull him out of our grasp. It pains me to enumerate these qualities, but enumerate them I must, that you might be forewarned and forearmed.

First and foremost, the teens (curse them) are remarkably tolerant of differences and are generally willing to give people a second chance. Don't believe the incendiary propaganda we disseminate through their fear-mongering politicians: racism, sexism, and prejudice in general are not particularly strong in the modern teen. He tends to accept others as they are and to allow them to express themselves as they see fit. This is not a good thing, but it can be channeled for our purposes. What you must be careful to do is to convince the teen that tolerance is the be-all and end-all of virtue. In this, the public schools have proved to be our willing accomplices. Let the teen view tolerance as an absolute good in the name of which any crime or immorality can be justified. The way to accomplish this is to separate tolerance from any concept of the innate dignity of man or of his shared fallen creatureliness and attach it instead to a weak-kneed relativism best summed up by the phrase "I like vanilla; you like chocolate." Let tolerance manifest itself not as a desire to lift up all men to a higher standard of dignity and morality but as yet another slogan for creating that lowest-common-denominator world that (as I told you earlier) is our real vision for modern America.

I said a moment ago that sexism is all but extinct among the modern teenager, though we have succeeded in fanning some residual misogyny through the efforts of our corps of rap artists (my, my, another oxymoron!). Still, among the more dangerous qualities of the teen (and of his society in general) is his willingness to allow real equality to girls and women. For thousands of years we have convinced the males of their species to keep most of their females ignorant and to stifle the exercise of their intellectual gifts and creative talents. Of course, to our dismay, those blasted women still managed to live meaningful lives, to shape their societies, and to pass on their legacy to their children, but only with great difficulty and at great cost to themselves. But now they are free, free to add their individual voices to that appalling symphony of humanity. I'm afraid there's no way to return to the good old days of oppression; however, if you will follow the steps of our new misinformation campaign, you just may inspire a deeper form of oppression.

First, convince them that the New Testament, the source of all real notions of equality, is actually the chief instigator of sexism and misogyny. Then, having cut them off from the Enemy's book, cause them to equate in their minds equality with sameness; indeed, make them redefine sexism to mean the belief that there are real, essential differences between the sexes (needless to say, they must not be allowed to read the book *Men Are from Mars, Women Are from Venus*). Make them believe, as we have already fooled their academics into believing, that gender is merely a social construct, that the only reason men and women are different is that they give boys trucks to play with and girls dolls to play with. If you are careful, you can actually convert their women into misogynistic feminists. No, I am not making another oxymoron. In the name of a radical, infernal egalitarianism that insists on deconstructing all gender differences, the modern female will actually suppress within herself her Enemy-given feminine qualities and lust after those very male qualities that she claims to despise. How fun it is to confuse and degrade them, and it is so easy. Such women, in the name of the egalitarian idol, will even leave their children to be raised by society, a great boon for us, since we have already quite thoroughly infiltrated the public sphere. And those poor, pathetic boys. Despite the fact that the majority of girls are still hungry for men with the courage and esteem to be true leaders, the boys (convinced, by us, that all girls are now feminists) are afraid to assert themselves in any way or take any leadership role. Even when they marry, they remain timid and indecisive, weakening their family structure and robbing them of that sexual game of active pursuit and passive surrender that the Enemy so loves but that we so hate. Yes, their egalitarian principles will allow for some modicum of intimacy, but it will not be the kind of intimacy the Enemy intended for marriage.

But all this talk of sex and gender reminds me of a third quality of the modern teen that causes me to seethe with anger. For a long, lovely generation we convinced the youth of America that sex on demand was not merely a right but that it would actually free them to be fuller, richer people. Satan be praised, what wonderful days those were: they copulated like dogs in the street, their passion reduced to that of insects while their lusts were as ravenous as goats. With one fell swoop, we succeeded in doing what three hundred years of Puritanism could never do: we completely divorced sex from intimacy. But today (curse them again), vast numbers of teens have bonded together in a program they call "True Love Waits." They vow to remain celibate until marriage and even wear rings to display (proudly) their repulsive vow. And they really go through with it! It simply sickens me: those weak, slavish-minded fools resisting the full force of our sexualized media blitz.

Still, a slight ray of hope remains. We at the TCP, after long hours of struggle, have come up with one counteroffensive to this resurgence of celibacy. Let them remain celibate if that is their desire, but at all costs convince them that the reason for their celibacy is not that sex is something pure and holy to be reserved for the sanctuary of the marriage bed, but that sex is dirty and shameful and bestial. Whisper in the ear of every girl who wears a True Love Waits ring that she is too good to be touched by some dirty male, that it would degrade her to be thought of as physically desirable. As for the boys, let them justify their own fears of intimacy and vulnerability in the name of some vague internal crusade of purity. Yes, turn them into little prudes; make them ashamed of their bodies with all its disgusting fluids and hormonal secretions. If you can carry it off, make them hate their own sexual nature and identity. Teach them to build self-protective walls around themselves. And always, always, always crush intimacy the moment it rears its ugly head. If you can transform celibacy from a positive virtue into a negative shield for guilt, fear, and isolation, then your victory will be complete!

I notice by the clock that my time runs short, but the urgency of the topic impels me to mention briefly two further qualities of the modern teen. The first, one that (I regret to admit) took us completely by surprise, is the growing desire among teens to volunteer their time and energy and even to run off on short-term missions. Such a concern for others can only disrupt our plans and leave an opening for the work of the Enemy. Still, you can modify the damage slightly by coaxing the teen to evaluate his charitable service solely in terms of how it affected *him*. Let him concentrate only on how the experience has made *him* a fuller person, while ignoring completely any impact on the lives of those he purportedly went out to serve. Egocentrism is a wonderful tool for lessening the harmful impacts of the Enemy's virtues. As long as the giver of charity remains trapped within his own narrow plans and his own limited self-consciousness, he will never really learn to love his neighbor as himself, for he will never be able to *see* his neighbor as himself.

Closely allied to this rise in volunteerism is a renewed desire on the part of young people to seek an authentic form of spirituality. Generally speaking, this is a bad thing. Better to confine all of them to a reductive naturalism than to risk opening their spirits to the voice of the Enemy. Still, because of our coordinated efforts to promote relativism in the schools and the media, it is not too difficult to convert their quest for the Enemy into a spiritual shopping spree. Allow them no spiritual discernment, no sense that there can be both a good form and a bad form of spirituality. Teach them that if words like *angel, prayer,* and *higher power* are used, then it must be good. Better yet, help them construct their own eclectic spirituality from bits and pieces of various religions and cultures. Divorce spirituality from Scripture, from doctrine, from morality, from accountability.

There is much more that I could tell you, but I see by the frantic waving of Chairman Mukrake that the dawn of the new millennium lies but a few moments away. It may shock you to hear this, but it gladdens my heart that so many humans up above are frantically waiting for the end of the world to fall upon them. Though such apocalyptic expectations have tended in the past to keep people focused on the Enemy, we have put a new twist on the matter. Today, more and more young people use such expectations as a handy excuse for irresponsibility. Rather than make difficult life choices or build lasting ties and relationships, they wait around for the end in a state of torpor. Even better, they spend inordinate time looking for us under every stone, while the Enemy gets virtually ignored. And besides, I do hope that none of you here this evening really believe all those lies about the Enemy's Son returning out of the sky and casting us all into the lake of fire. Propaganda, nothing but propaganda. Dominion is ours, my fellow tempters, and it is the teenagers who shall pave the way. Indeed, a little child *shall* lead them, but it shall be to a mountain of mediocrity: colorless, sexless, passionless, mindless. And from every hilltop shall rise the Noise, louder and louder till every thought, every dream, every desire is finally and irrevocably crushed. To thee, O coming pandemonium, I raise my glass!

LEWIS ON EDUCATION
AND THE ARTS:
A BIBLIOGRAPHICAL ESSAY

I n this bibliographical essay, I will assess some of the main biographies of Lewis, discuss those works by Lewis that most touch on the arts and education, and survey some of the books about Lewis that offer insight into these two areas.

In Lewis biography, the two extremes are best represented by *C. S. Lewis: A Biography* by Roger Lancelyn Green and Walter Hooper (Harcourt Brace Jovanovich, 1974) and *C. S. Lewis: A Biography* by A. N. Wilson (Fawcett Columbine, 1990). The former was written by two close friends of Lewis: the first a pupil of Lewis; the second his personal secretary in the closing months of his life and the indefatigable editor of most of his shorter works. As such, it tends to idealize Lewis and to brush over controversial issues (like his strange relationship with Mrs. Moore). Still, it offers a good read and brings both Lewis and his works alive. Fans of Lewis will particularly appreciate the inclusion of the diary entries that Green took when he traveled to Greece with Lewis and Joy.

The latter biography is far more critical and does not shy away from Lewis's darker side. Indeed, it consciously and unapologetically sets out to dispel the Lewis-as-saint approach that Green and Hooper adopt in their biography. As such, it achieves a more objective view of Lewis than does the Green-Hooper biography, but by so doing lacks the charm and vitality of their work. At the end of Wilson's biography, I know a great deal *about* Lewis, but I feel that I *know* him better at the end of Green-Hooper's.

There is also something unsettling about Wilson's approach to Lewis the defender of Christianity. Wilson's obvious distaste for Lewis's brand of apologetics has the result of keeping the core Lewis—he whose faith in a historic God-man completely transformed both himself and his work—forever at arm's length. In addition, it leads Wilson to make the untenable argument that the real, mature Lewis is the one who wrote *A Grief Observed*; all those early, cocky apologetical works were the products of an emotional and intellectual immaturity. To me it is no mystery why Wilson, along with many others in the liberal wings of academia and the church, would adopt this view: *A Grief Observed*, though brilliant and sincere, makes few demands on the often noncreedal faith of the modern reader; *Mere Christianity* and the other early works force us to come face to face with the claims of Christ and the Bible. Wilson seems intent in his biography on "defusing" Lewis, on making him safe for the modern agnostic who wants religion without accountability and a faith that allows us to dismiss any doctrine that, to our modern mindset, seems archaic, narrow, or dogmatic.

Is it, then, necessary for the student of Lewis to read Wilson? Necessary, no; but worthwhile, yes. It is good to be reminded that Lewis had his flaws and that he wasn't always as congenial as we like to imagine him; it is also good to remember that, even if Wilson *is* prejudiced against Lewis the apologist, then so were most of Lewis's colleagues and fellow Inklings. In addition, the Wilson biography holds one great advantage for American readers: it is more careful than Green and Hooper to explain such "Briticisms" as the tutorial system at Oxford and Cambridge and the English public school system.

In between these two books comes a third that, to my mind, is the finest available biography of Lewis: *Jack: A Life of C. S. Lewis* by George Sayer (Crossway Books, 1994; originally published in 1988 under the title *Jack: C. S. Lewis and His Times*). Like Green, Sayer was a onetime pupil and longtime friend of C. S. Lewis. His book combines the personal insight of the Green-Hooper biography with the critical objectivity of the Wilson biography. He is more frank and open about Lewis's struggles than Green-Hooper while yet refraining, as Wilson does not, from simplistic, reductive Freudian readings of his religious work. In the afterword to the 1994 edition, Sayer persuasively refutes Wilson's controversial contention that Lewis and Joy had sexual relations between their civil and church weddings and defends Lewis in general against revisionist attacks on his character and his psyche.

Another biography that inhabits the middle ground between Green-Hooper and Wilson is *The Narnian: The Life and Imagination of C. S. Lewis* by Alan Jacobs (HarperSan Francisco, 2005). Jacobs's well-researched biography gives us more critical insight into Lewis's academic works than do the other biographies, and he focuses especially on those events in Lewis's life that most influenced his writing of the Chronicles. Indeed, lovers of the Chronicles must read this biography, for in it, Jacobs convincingly argues that it is the imaginative, rather than the rational, side of Lewis that offers the key to his character. In a sense, this biography shows how the arts and imagination helped shape Lewis. Jacobs does a good job defending Lewis from many of Wilson's critiques, but he has a disturbing (and trendy) tendency to downplay Lewis the apologist and to "overapologize" for Lewis's supposed sexism.

Many other biographies of Lewis exist and continue to be written, but I think these four are the best. Still, I would recommend several other books that offer partial biographies of Lewis that are relevant to his thoughts on educations and the arts. Humphrey Carpenter's *The Inklings: C. S. Lewis, J. R. R. Tolkien, Charles Williams, and Their Friends* (Houghton Mifflin, 1979) offers a well-conceived "collective biography" of Lewis, Tolkien, and Williams that provides its reader with the rare opportunity to eavesdrop on three great literary minds as they encourage and critique one another. Diana Glyer's *The Company They Keep: C. S. Lewis and J. R. R. Tolkien as Writers in Community* (Kent State UP, 2008) documents how the Inklings worked as a writing group and how their encouragement and criticism of each other's work exerted a strong and lasting influence on all of them. Colin Duriez provides much insight into the artistically fruitful friendship between Lewis and Tolkien in *Tolkien and C. S. Lewis: The Gift of Friendship* (Paulist Press, 2003). Joel Heck's *Irrigating Deserts: C. S. Lewis on Education* (Concordia Academic Press, 2005) offers a unique look at Lewis the student and Lewis the professor. *C. S. Lewis: Speaker and Teacher*, edited by Carolyn Keefe (Zondervan, 1971), offers seven freestanding essays/reminiscences that give insight into Lewis's approach and style in the classroom and on the platform. *Reading the Classics with C. S. Lewis*, edited by Thomas L. Martin (Paternoster Press, 2001), while not a biography, offers a very helpful collection of essays on Lewis's interactions with classic writers. It not only offers essays dealing with specific authors (Shakespeare and Milton) and literary periods (Renaissance, Romantic, Victorian) and genres (fantasy, science fiction, children's literature), but also provides a strong sense of Lewis in the classroom and the library.

Of course, Lewis himself wrote both a spiritual autobiography, *Surprised by Joy*, and an allegorical autobiography, *The Pilgrim's Regress*. Both works detail his intellectual journey toward faith, focusing on the many twentieth-century "isms" that competed for his allegiance and temporarily impeded his movement toward Christianity.

Lewis's letters are also available in numerous editions, but the ones that give the most insight into his early formative years and his overall personality are those anthologized in *They Stand Together: The Letters of C. S. Lewis to Arthur Greeves, 1914–1963* (edited by Walter Hooper and published by Collins, 1979). True to the small-talk-hating Lewis, these letters waste little time on personal details, devoting most of their space to spontaneous, loving critiques of whatever book Lewis was reading at the time. Fans of Lewis will enjoy discovering the young Lewis's obsession with well-bound books and Wagner and will enjoy a knowing laugh as the pre-Christian Lewis teases Greeves for his faith. Though casual readers of Lewis can skip this one, anyone who *really* wants to know him *must* read this collection; it does a better job than any of Lewis's many biographers at capturing the pre-Oxford Lewis. And yes, remarkably, all five hundred pages are truly worth reading! One last note: if you do pick up this collection, make sure to read carefully all the letters that Lewis wrote during 1930: that vital year during which Lewis's newfound theism was slowly developing into a creedal Christianity. In these letters, one can literally watch as Lewis's mind struggles with the impending reality of the Christian faith and with the need to mortify his lifelong desire to be a celebrated poet.

Lovers of Narnia may also wish to consult *Letters to Children*, edited by Lyle W. Dorsett and Marjorie Lamp Mead (Macmillan, 1985), for the scattered insights it affords into the Chronicles, especially the character and person of Aslan.

For more personal insight into Lewis, see James T. Como's *C. S. Lewis at the Breakfast Table and Other Reminiscences* (Macmillan, 1979), which includes a smorgasbord of essays written by those who knew Lewis best. I offer biographical overviews of Lewis in a twelve-lecture series I produced with the Teaching Company (www.teach12.com), *The Life and Writings of C. S. Lewis* (2000), and in the first chapter of my book *Lewis Agonistes: How C. S. Lewis Can Train Us to Wrestle with the Modern and Postmodern World* (Broadman & Holman, 2003). The lecture series also provides an extensive annotated bibliography of works by and about Lewis, while chapters 3 and 5 of *Lewis Agonistes* discuss how Lewis can help us wrestle with the challenges posed by the modern resurgence of neo-paganism and the postmodern deconstruction of the arts and of language. I offer further C. S. Lewis resources on my personal webpage: www.Loumarkos. com.

Below I have listed books and essays by Lewis in which he discusses issues relevant to education and the arts. I begin with the major popular works; as these exist in numerous editions, I have only included the original year of publication. I then follow with the lesser-known academic works and essay collections; for these I provide publisher and copyright date. The first list is grouped chronologically, the second alphabetically.

I have put an asterisk (*) by those works that are most central to an understanding of Lewis's views on education and the arts.

Major Popular Works

The Pilgrim's Regress: An Allegorical Apology for Christianity, Reason, and Romanticism (1933). This was the first book Lewis published after his conversion to Christianity in 1931. It is modeled after Bunyan's *Pilgrim's Progress* but is really an allegorical account of Lewis's conversion. It follows Lewis's persona (John) as he travels from the legalistic Puritania to true Christianity. He is led on his journey by an unaccountable sense of joy (or desire) for which he can find no true fulfillment. In seeking the proper source and end of this joy (Christ and heaven), John takes many wrong turns, falling into such philosophical dead ends as hedonism, stoicism, idealism, materialism, and scientism. Though the allegorical characters are wonderfully drawn and there is much insight into the failure of post-Enlightenment philosophy to speak to man's deepest needs, the middle sections bog down and are hard to follow. Those without some working knowledge of philosophical terms and schools may get more lost than John himself! Still, this work offers powerful insight into those very "isms" that have pushed both education and the arts off track and, at times, have converted them into forces that crush rather than uplift the human spirit and impede its journey toward truth.

The Space Trilogy: Out of the Silent Planet (1938), *Perelandra* (1943), and *That Hideous Strength* (1945). Lewis's attempt to bring together science fiction and Christian allegory; based on the fascinating assumption that journeys into space are best handled in spiritual (rather than scientific) terms. Though all three novels offer a subtle defense of medieval notions of beauty, truth, and hierarchy, the novel that is most relevant to education and the arts is the third. Written just two years after *The Abolition of Man*, *That Hideous Strength* fictionalizes what might happen if England were truly to throw out all higher standards of goodness, truth, and beauty and attempt to build a purely scientific, purely rational utopia. Central to Lewis's critique of modern theories of education and the arts is a scene in which the evil forces attempt to corrupt the soul of the protagonist by deconstructing his understanding of the good, the true, and the beautiful. The novel also includes a satiric exposé of university politics.

The Screwtape Letters (1942; with later editions including *"Screwtape Proposes a Toast"). Though this witty series of letters from a senior devil to a junior devil detailing the fine art of temptation does not deal directly with either education or the arts, it does discuss how the Devil has used the search for the historical Jesus and the historical point of view as devices to ensure that modern students will be insulated from the truth claims not only of the Bible but also of the Great Books of the Western tradition. More generally, this book shows in numerous subtle ways how it is the Devil, not God, who is antireason. Most, though not all, editions of *The Screwtape Letters* contain a later essay Lewis wrote titled "Screwtape Proposes a Toast." This essay, in which Lewis critiques modern education, is a must read for its insight into how egalitarianism in our schools has disrupted true learning and threatens to rob democracy of what it most needs: a stable base of educated citizens who can read, write, and think critically.

The Abolition of Man; or Reflections on Education with Special Reference to the Teaching of English in the Upper Forms of Schools (1943). This is one of Lewis's most difficult works but is absolutely essential reading not only for those interested or involved in teaching but also for all those concerned about the direction that Western civilization has been heading in for the last century. Basically, the book predicts what the outcome will be for a society that trains its youth in accordance with the principles of relativism and ethical subjectivism. It has affinities to *The Pilgrim's Regress* in its critique of post-Enlightenment thought and to *That Hideous Strength* and other dystopic novels (*1984, Brave New World*, etc.) in its sober prophecy of what the future holds. This book includes a lengthy appendix in which Lewis offers a cross-cultural list of ethical statements culled from the main philosophical and religious texts of the past to show that the moral impetus behind the Ten Commandments and the Sermon on the Mount are not unique or relative but form a central core of accepted, a priori values (what Lewis calls the "Tao") that undergird our moral standards and behavior. Lewis references this list in the first chapter of *Mere Christianity*.

The Great Divorce: A Dream (1946). Though this imaginative study of heaven and hell does not deal directly with either the arts or education, it provides us with the case study of a damned painter whose original love for painting no longer draws him upward to heavenly beauty but has become a mere end in itself, a dead form that has lost its soul and reason for being. More generally, Lewis illustrates in this book that while hell represents a shriveled and barren state of mind, heaven embodies true reality, a reality more real than any earthly philosophy or school or work of art.

Miracles: A Preliminary Study (1947). Though not about education per se, the impassioned defense that Lewis mounts of the reality of miracles and the supernatural makes this work of apologetics important reading for educators who would challenge the academy's a priori rejection of miracles.

*The Chronicles of Narnia: The Lion, the Witch and the Wardrobe; *Prince Caspian; The Voyage of the Dawn Treader; * The Silver Chair; The Horse and His Boy; The Magician's Nephew;* and *The Last Battle* (one per year from 1950 to 1956). These are probably Lewis's best-known and best-loved works, magical tales for children and adults of all ages that work equally well as pure fantasy or as Christian allegory. Just as the beauty of Narnia that Lewis captures in these novels offers a much-needed antidote to the growing ascendancy of ugliness, so the medieval notions of hierarchy and chivalry that he champions offer a countervision to the modern idolatry of egalitarianism. Although all seven novels contain ideas and arguments that embody, in literary form, Lewis's views on education, I would highlight two of them. *Prince Caspian* shows us how modern revisionist history can squelch imagination and pervert the soul. *The Silver Chair* not only provides a satirical picture of modern education theory run amuck in the experimental school that Eustace and Jill attend but also exposes, in the scene when the Emerald Witch attempts to "teach" the children and Puddleglum that Narnia does not exist, the attempts of modern secular educators to reduce religious belief to fairy tales and wish fulfillment.

Mere Christianity (1952). Although this, Lewis's greatest work of apologetics, does not address education or the arts directly, it discusses at length the importance of the classical and theological virtues (prudence, justice, fortitude, and temperance; faith, hope, and charity). It also discusses the central role that Christian morality plays in the smooth running of society.

Surprised by Joy: The Shape of My Early Life (1955). This is Lewis's spiritual autobiography. Like *The Pilgrim's Regress*, it traces how Lewis, in seeking a final object for his early, mystical experiences of joy, eventually found his way into the harbor of orthodox Christianity. As much of this book follows Lewis as he navigates his way through a number of negative educational experiences, it is essential reading for those seeking to understand and assess Lewis's own thoughts on education. It does a particularly good job of demonstrating that a true reading of the classics cannot help but open our minds and hearts to greater spiritual realities.

Till We Have Faces: A Myth Retold (1956). This, Lewis's best-written and conceived novel, retells the myth of Cupid and Psyche (see Apuleius's *The Golden Ass* IV–VI for the original story) in such a way as to weave together Greek myth and Christian allegory. The tale is told in the first person by one of the "ugly sisters" of the lovely Psyche and contains remarkable psychological depth and insight into the virtuous and vicious side of human nature. By telling his tale through the lips of a woman who is physically ugly, Lewis is enabled to explore notions of inner and outer beauty in a sincere, sensitive, and subtle way.

Academic Works and Essays

Christian Reflections (Eerdmans, 1967). In the opening two essays of this fine collection (a sort-of companion volume to *God in the Dock*), Lewis explores the relationship between literature, culture, and Christianity. Other subjects covered that are relevant to education and the arts are the poison of subjectivism and the dangers of historicism and biblical criticism.

The Discarded Image: An Introduction to Medieval and Renaissance Literature (Cambridge UP, 1994). Lewis's last book (originally published in 1964) offers a fascinating study of the medieval and Renaissance worldview that takes up that era's conception of the entire cosmos, from the heavens to the earth, from man to nature, from the body to the soul. Anyone wishing to understand and appreciate fully Lewis's thoughts on education and the arts must read this book, for it takes us back to a time when Western man related to the cosmos not as an object to be studied but as a poem or a woman to be loved. Could we revive that sense in our own modern age, it would take us a great way toward restoring our lost appreciation of order, harmony, and beauty and renewing our schools as places where students are taught and encouraged to journey toward higher truth.

An Experiment in Criticism (Cambridge UP, 1961). In this low-key, accessible work of literary criticism, Lewis sets forth his own eclectic, antitheoretical theory of what impels people to read literature. Though a minor work, it represents an attempt by Lewis the professor to rescue education from arcane and politically motivated theories that have cut readers off from the true wisdom that the Great Books have to teach us.

God in the Dock: Essays on Theology and Ethics (Eerdmans, 1970). Though this excellent collection of essays focuses mostly on apologetics, it touches on issues that are relevant to education. Lewis's meditations on the ongoing debate between science and religion, naturalism and supernaturalism, for example, offer much guidance to modern educators who must decide whether or not Darwinism should be taught in our schools as a proven fact or a flawed theory.

On Stories, and Other Essays on Literature (HBJ, 1982). This collection provides rare insight into how and why Lewis wrote The Chronicles of Narnia and The Space Trilogy. It also contains Lewis's reflections on the nature and function of children's literature, on the distinction between popular and serious literature, on the various subgenres of science fiction, and on the works of J. R. R. Tolkien, George Orwell, Charles Williams, and H. Rider Haggard. Finally, it contains a seminal, must-read essay, "A Reply to Professor Haldane," in which Lewis defends his Space Trilogy, clarifies the various ideologies he was attacking in *That Hideous Strength* and *The Abolition of Man*, and explains why he felt democracy was the best form of government for a fallen world. Many of the essays in this collection also appear in *Of Other Worlds: Essays and Stories* (HBJ, 1966).

The Personal Heresy: A Controversy (Oxford UP, 1939). This is one of Lewis's earliest works of criticism. It documents a debate with E. M. W. Tillyard in which Lewis takes the position—one shared by such American New Critics as John Crowe Ransom, W. K. Wimsatt, and Cleanth Brooks—that works of art should not be evaluated on the basis of the personality of their creator. Here, as in his much later *An Experiment in*

Criticism, Lewis the professor tries to keep our focus on literature itself. This book, long out of print, has recently been reissued.

A Preface to Paradise Lost (Oxford UP, 1961; originally published 1942). In this challenging but accessible study of Milton's *Paradise Lost* and the epic tradition out of which it sprang, Lewis the professor succeeds in weaving a spell of academic/literary magic. In direct contrast to modern critics who would teach us to stand in judgment on Milton and his beliefs, Lewis allows his reader to experience and understand *Paradise Lost* as its poet and the people of his age would have seen it. This work, like most of his other academic works, also offers a needed corrective against that typical modern arrogance that says our view of things is innately superior to that of all previous ages.

Present Concerns (HBJ, 1986). Though not one of the major collections, this book contains three essays that are essential reading for those who wish to gauge Lewis's views on modern education: "Equality," "Is English Doomed?" and "Democratic Education." These essays are best read in conjunction with "Screwtape Proposes a Toast."

Selected Literary Essays (Cambridge UP, 1969; including * "De Descriptione Temporum"). If you want to see Lewis the literary critic in action, this collection of essays is the best place to start. It contains essays on Chaucer, Shakespeare, Bunyan, Austen, Shelley, Sir Walter Scott, William Morris, Kipling, and others. More important it contains the lecture Lewis gave to inaugurate his tenure as chair of medieval and Renaissance literature at Cambridge: "De Descriptione Temporum." In this lecture, Lewis breaks down modern "chronological snobbery" that would erect a wall between the dark and ignorant Middle Ages and the enlightened Renaissance. He also refers famously to himself as a dinosaur, as an old European man who is more in touch with the world of Dante, Chaucer, Shakespeare, and Milton than our own.

The Weight of Glory and Other Addresses (Macmillan, 1980). This is a revised and expanded edition of a collection initially published by Lewis in 1949. It contains Lewis's greatest sermon on the nature of heaven ("The Weight of Glory"), a timeless meditation that gets to the heart of our human yearning for true beauty. In addition, the collection includes a second seminal essay ("Transpositions") that not only adds further detail to Lewis's conception of heaven but also fleshes out his central notion of joy and his Platonic, antinaturalist faith that lower things are reflections of higher things. Finally, it offers two complementary essays ("The Inner Ring" and "Membership") that not only read like rough drafts of *That Hideous Strength* but also explore the fascinating paradoxes of a man who championed loyalty to one's friends but despised all cliques, who advocated democracy yet was our century's greatest apologist for medieval hierarchy.

———

Those interested in exploring Lewis's thoughts on education and the arts would do well to begin with the ever-growing number of studies devoted to The Chronicles of Narnia. Paul Ford's *Companion to Narnia* (HarperSanFrancisco, 1980, with many reprints) offers a complete, alphabetically organized, fully cross-referenced guide to all seven novels. Kathryn Lindskoog's *Journey into Narnia* (Hope Publishing House, 1997) unpacks the Christian themes and ethical lessons that Lewis smuggles into his novels. Peter Schakel's *Reading with the Heart: The Way into Narnia* (Eerdmans, 1979) uncovers the archetypal patterns and images that underlie the Chronicles. Michael Ward's *Planet Narnia: The Seven Heavens in the Imagination of C. S. Lewis* (Oxford UP, 2008) offers a brilliant and fresh reading of the Chronicles that argues that Lewis keyed each of the seven novels to the seven medieval "planets" (Moon, Mercury, Venus, Sun, Mars, Jupiter, Saturn) and their particular influences. (This study is best read in conjunction with *The Discarded Image* and The Space Trilogy.) More recent works (most inspired by the 2005 film release of *The Lion, the Witch and the Wardrobe*) that seek to draw out the Christian meanings of the Chronicles include *A Family Guide to Narnia: Biblical Truths in C. S. Lewis's The Chronicles of Narnia* by Christin Ditchfield; *Into the Wardrobe: C. S. Lewis and the Narnia Chronicles* by David C. Downing; *Meeting God in The Lion, the Witch and the Wardrobe* by Sara McLaughlin; *A Field Guide to Narnia* by Colin Duriez; *A Reader's Guide Through the Wardrobe: Exploring C. S. Lewis's Classic Story* by Leland

Ryken and Marjorie Lamp Mead; and *Aslan's Call: Finding Our Way to Narnia* by Mark Eddy Smith. In 2010, a new study of the Chronicles of Narnia was published that offers a clear and concise analysis of the spiritual architecture that undergirds each of the Chronicles: Will Vaus's *The Hidden Story of Narnia* (Winged Lion Press).

For help in understanding and interpreting The Space Trilogy, the best resource is David C. Downing's *Planets in Peril: A Critical Study of C. S. Lewis's Ransom Trilogy* (The University of Massachusetts Press, 1992). In each chapter of this well-organized and thoroughly researched book, Downing takes up a different aspect of the Trilogy (theology, medievalism, literary allusions, autobiography) and then skillfully weaves that aspect (or theme) through each of the three books. The reader emerges from Downing's book with a rich and multifaceted understanding of the Trilogy.

As for *Till We Have Faces*, there is no better guide than Peter J. Schakel's *Reason and Imagination in C. S. Lewis: A Study of* Till We Have Faces (Eerdmans, 1984). In part I, Schakel surveys the novel chapter by chapter, first giving a quick synopsis of the plot and then analyzing relevant themes and images and explaining allusions to Greek mythology and philosophy. In part II, Schakel looks again at the novel, but from the perspective of Lewis's other works. He chooses a representative work from each of the decades in which Lewis wrote—the '20s through the '60s—and compares and contrasts its treatment of themes and concerns that are key to *Till We Have Faces*. By so doing, Schakel helps us see how Lewis's understanding of the merits and limitations of reason and imagination developed over his lifetime.

Some general, standard studies of Lewis's fiction include Evan K. Gibson's *C. S. Lewis: Spinner of Tales* (Christian University Press, 1980); Thomas Howard's *The Achievements of C. S. Lewis: A Reading of His Fiction* (Harold Shaw, 1980; reissued in England in 1987 by Churchman Publishing, under the title *C. S. Lewis: Man of Letters: A Reading of His Fiction*); Peter Schakel and Charles Huttar's *Word and Story in C. S. Lewis* (University of Missouri Press, 1991); Lionel Adey's *C. S. Lewis: Writer, Dreamer, and Mentor* (Eerdmans, 1998); and Richard Purtill's *Lord of the Elves and Eldils: Fantasy and Philosophy in C. S. Lewis and J. R. R.*

Tolkien (second edition from Ignatius Press, 2006). The best recent book to take up Lewis the fiction writer is Peter Schakel's *Imagination and the Arts in C. S. Lewis: Journeying to Narnia and Other Worlds* (University of Missouri Press, 2002).

Four books that are not specifically about Lewis's fiction but that nevertheless offer insights that illuminate the Chronicles and/or The Space Trilogy are Corbin Scott Carnell's *Bright Shadow of Reality: C. S. Lewis and the Feeling Intellect* (Eerdmans, 1974); Paul L. Holmer's *C. S. Lewis: The Shape of His Faith and Thought* (Harper & Row, 1976); Gilbert Meilaender's *The Taste for the Other: The Social and Ethical Thought of C. S. Lewis* (Eerdmans, 1978); and Leanne Payne's *Real Presence: The Holy Spirit in the Works of C. S. Lewis* (Cornerstone Books, 1979).

Those who need help breaking the allegorical code of *The Pilgrim's Regress* and identifying the many "isms" that it critiques should consult Kathryn Lindskoog's *Finding the Landlord: A Guidebook to C. S. Lewis's Pilgrim's Regress* (Cornerstone Books, 1995).

Most helpful of all, those who wish not only to understand *The Abolition of Man* but also to assess its predictive power must consult Peter Kreeft's *C. S. Lewis for the Third Millennium: Six Essays on* The Abolition of Man (Ignatius Press, 1994). More than just a study of *The Abolition of Man*, Kreeft's book pieces together all of Lewis's scattered comments on history, ethics, and progress. What is more, Kreeft, as he wends his way through the Lewis canon, adds his own carefully thought-out analysis of the direction Western civilization has been taking over the last century. And Kreeft does so in a prose style that is as lucid and witty as that of Lewis himself. Fans of *The Abolition of Man*, as well as those who share Lewis's (and Kreeft's) concern about where our culture is heading, should definitely read this book.

Finally, as Lewis's thoughts on education and the arts often contrast sharply with those of Sigmund Freud, much of value can be garnered from Armand Nicholi's *The Question of God: C. S. Lewis and Sigmund Freud Debate God, Love, Sex, and the Meaning of Life* (Free Press, 2002). Though Dr. Nicholi, who based his book on a popular class that he teaches at Harvard, does not focus specifically on education or the arts, the issues he covers in his book help provide a framework for Lewis's beliefs concerning the good, the true, and the beautiful. The book was later followed by a two-part PBS special, *The Question of God*, which alternates back and forth between footage that compares and contrasts the biographies and beliefs of C. S. Lewis and Sigmund Freud and includes a no-holds-barred roundtable discussion of the issues raised by the works of Lewis and Freud.